MENTAL AMERICA

72 HOURS WITH AN EMERGENCY ROOM CRISIS COUNSELOR

STEWART SWAIN

Copyright © 2024 by Stewart Swain.

All rights reserved. No part of this book may be reproduced in whole or in part without written permission from the publisher or author, except by reviewers who may quote brief excerpts in connection with a review in a newspaper, magazine, or electronic publication; nor may any part of this book be reproduced, stored in a retrieval system, or transmitted in any form or by any means electronic, mechanical, photocopying, recording, or other, without written permission from the publisher or author.

Stewart Swain Productions/Mental America
Printed in the United States of America

Although every precaution has been taken to verify the accuracy of the information contained herein, the author and publisher assume no responsibility for any errors or omissions. No liability is assumed for damages that may result from the use of information contained within.

Mental America/Stewart Swain -- First Edition

ISBN 9798883306913 Print Edition

CONTENTS

One 1

Two 17

Three 29

Four 45

Five 61

Six 75

Seven 89

Eight 99

Nine 111

Ten 127

Eleven 141

Twelve 153

Thirteen 167

To Jason

The truth doesn't exist.
It's all about who presents the best argument.
The best argument turns into the truth.

ONE

"So, Bob, if you want me to release you tonight and not send you to a mental hospital, you'd better tell me what happened?"

Bob is at a loss for words. He pulls the blanket a little closer; I see fear in his eyes, replacing the anger he's been showing everyone in the ER for the last hour. I look down at my pen and start to dismantle it. Bob is watching. If I can't take notes, then any statement is off the record. It's an old trick. I use it often. I hold the ink to the light, examining the contents. I shake it like a thermometer. Seemingly lost in my own world, I start searching my pockets for something.

"Anyone need coffee?"

It's one of the emergency room nurses. She looks down at my pen scattered in pieces on my clipboard. I'm sitting in a chair next to the patient. He appears comfortable, reclined in a hospital bed covered with a blanket. The nurse smiles at my pen. She knows my tricks. I look at my watch: 11:00 PM.

"Sure, why not. It's still early," I reply. "Bob, do you want some coffee?"

He has trouble with the decision. According to his family, he lost his mind tonight and attacked his son-in-law. Six family members are in the lobby waiting. I already interviewed them, so I have at least half of the story.

"I'll get some in a few minutes, Sarah. Thanks."

Her question was in code. What she was really saying was it looks like you're going to be here all night. According to the triage nurse, the fire department is running another call for a homicidal patient. I'd rather talk to a homicidal patient any day. I frequently feel homicidal. I can relate to those patients better. Suicide just wouldn't be as interesting. Sarah taps the door jamb and walks away. I look at Bob. He's watching me assemble my pen.

"What did you say your name was?" he asks, trying to look at me through filthy glasses. I pause, wondering why no one in his family helps him with his glasses.

"My name is Stewart. Here, give me your glasses. They're really dirty."

I pull a handkerchief from my pocket. I think it's clean, but I'm not sure. I carefully unfold it on my lap. Bob is watching me again. It's just another trick—present as meek and subservient and patients will tell you anything. That's why I always sit in a chair and fidget with my pen when I interview the mentally ill. You have to gain their trust if you are going to learn anything.

Bob gives me his glasses without much hesitation. He is letting his guard down. In large measure it's because I haven't accused him of anything, unlike his family. I try to be as neutral as possible during a patient interview, so I can get as much information as I need to make my decision. I introduce myself as just Stewart, and I say the ER doctor wanted me to talk to them. The truth is the ER doctor can't wait for me to make a decision whether to release the patient or send them to a psychiatric hospital for further evaluation. The doctors that work in this emergency room don't hurry me for a decision, though. They let me take my time. They know I'm good. Plus, medical doctors hate treating mental illness. It's a subject briefly examined in medical school. Everyone figures the psychiatrists will study and treat mental illness. The problem is there are very few psychiatrists.

That's where I come in. I'm part of a crisis team, a small group of mental health counselors working in the ER treating homicidal, suicidal, and substance abuse patients. This is just one emergency room serving one county in one state anywhere in America, and the public would be amazed if they knew how many mentally ill patients rolled through their local hospitals every day. Acute mental illness is an epidemic, it's another pandemic, it's highly contagious, and it's been around since the beginning of civilization. But here's something really hard to swallow: there's no solution to the problem, and there never will be.

"See if that helps, Bob."

He puts his glasses back on and smiles. The smile is painful and unfamiliar. Bob is so used to psychosis that the natural act of smiling has eroded from his memory. His family tried to convince me he was crazy, all six of them at once, but I'm not convinced. I conducted the interview in a quiet waiting room normally closed to evening admissions. I wanted full control of the conversation, no distractions. They all sat in a row of seats watching me as I dismantled my pen and asked pointed questions. Bob is an old man. He's 72 years old.

"Do you remember attacking your son-in-law, Bob? What's his name, anyhow?"

He pauses. "Michael."

I pretend to remember. "Oh, that's right."

"My family says I'm crazy. It's not true." He looks straight at me this time. "Are you a doctor?" I hear that question all the time. To avoid a long discussion, I respond with an easy answer.

"I'm a counselor. Dr. Mattia asked me to talk with you."

Counselor, psychologist, psychiatrist? What matters is I'm the guy who can send you home or send you to a mental hospital for the next three weeks. He weighs my answer carefully.

"He put his arms around me and tried to hold me down."

"Who tried to hold you down?"

"Michael, my son-in-law."

"So, why was he trying to hold you down, Bob?"

This is obviously a hard question for Bob to answer. If he can pull it together enough to give me a good reason, then I may not have to send Bob to Oakwood Hospital, the state mental hospital two hours away. It's a huge facility that treats acute mental illness as well as chronic psychotic disorders. Some of the patients are permanent residents. This is Bob's big chance to formulate an alibi, whether factual or fictitious. I look at my watch. It's getting close to midnight. A cup of strong coffee sounds good. I'm about to excuse myself and take a break when he finally answers.

"I didn't want to come to the hospital. I was afraid I would get locked up."

His voice quivers. I suddenly feel a little sorry for him. An old man, a grandfather, shouldn't have to face such an undignified interrogation, against his will, at midnight, at the local emergency room.

"Why were you afraid we might lock you up, Bob?"

The conversation sounds so elementary, but when you are talking to homicidal, suicidal, and patients overdosed on drugs, simplicity is best. I hear the automatic doors to the ambulance bay slide open. A security guard goes to meet the new arrival. The repetitive beep, beep, beep of the ambulance back-up signal wafts through the emergency room. No one bothers to look up.

"I…"

Bob wants my full attention now. He leans forward, clutching the disposable blanket. I lean toward him because I hate to miss the crucial statements and sordid confessions. So often tears and sobbing distort the interview. I always want to say something like, "Speak up for God's sake, this is getting really interesting!"

"It's really scary. I can't remember things."

And he's done talking. That's all I get out of him. He sheds a tear and is quick to wipe it away. Bob is a proud man. He's nicely dressed in a flannel button-down shirt tucked neatly into khaki pants, accessorized with penny loafers and a matching belt. I'm sure he dressed himself before coming to the hospital. He's thin but appears well nourished and healthy.

I stand up and put my hand on his shoulder. My clipboard and pen are at my side. He holds his breath, waiting for my response. I look at the stainless-steel medical tray with bloody gauze and the remains of an IV start—sterile tubing and a syringe cap. Bob has a hep-lock IV in his arm, just in case he needs emergency medication. One of the nurses already drew blood and sent it to the lab to rule out blood sugar abnormalities, metabolic anomalies, and alcohol ingestion. A urine drug screen was ordered, too. I have the lab results on my clipboard. I knew he was sober before we started the conversation.

"Try not to be afraid. It's a common disorder. I'll see what I can do, Bob. I'll talk to Dr. Mattia."

I leave the examination room and smile at the charge nurse. She nods her head. Body language is 90% of staff communication in an emergency room. I immediately go to the break room hoping to find some cold pizza to eat with my coffee. There's a *COPS* rerun on the television. Everyone that works in an emergency room is an adrenaline junkie. You just can't get enough once it starts flowing. I was a paramedic in an earlier life, and I worked a few years as a fireman. A really good adrenaline rush makes your hair stand up, your senses redline, and it leaves you with a metallic taste in the back of your throat. I get the same sensation when I'm kayaking by myself in a swamp, and I feel like I'm about to be eaten by alligators.

Back in the ER, I find Dr. Mattia reading internet articles about erectile dysfunction. I make a mental note to laugh later but try my best to ignore the screen. Maybe the information is for one of the patients.

"What do you have?" He doesn't look up.

"The guy in Bed Thirteen is alert and oriented, times four. No suicidal ideations. No homicidal ideations. His entire extended family is here, and they want him locked up."

So far, Dr. Mattia knows all this. He interviewed Bob first before calling me for a further assessment. Emergency mental health treatment varies from hospital to hospital based on the resources available. Some emergency rooms have full-time psychiatrists to treat acutely mentally ill patients. Those hospitals usually have a floor dedicated to mental illness complete with full-time security and long-term therapy. Other emergency rooms, like the one I work in, either release the patient to go home with a family member or transfer them to a mental hospital, sometimes hours away, transportation courtesy of local law enforcement. And don't think for a minute that the mental hospitals are happily waiting for your phone call and the next psychiatric patient. Mental hospitals are packed full. The whole mental health system is saturated with patients. It's difficult on a good day getting a mental hospital to accept your patient. It takes hours of phone conversations and a pile of paperwork.

Dr. Mattia nods. He leans back in his chair and adds a short laugh. Sarcasm is a universal language, and Dr. Mattia has a limited sense of humor.

"The guy in Four says his chest pain isn't going away," one of the nurses tells him as she rushes by.

"Order labs," he responds.

Out of the corner of my eye I see my next patient roll in with handcuffs and a police escort. Two paramedics are wheeling the gurney. The patient looks intoxicated and pissed off.

"Twelve?" asks the charge nurse.

Dr. Mattia simply points to the room, showing his approval. Emergency room doctors are incredible at multitasking. I sometimes wonder if Dr. Mattia is tasking at all. He's not one to work fast.

I see a pause in the drama, a momentary lapse in the chaos where I can inject my recommendation. Wired on cold pizza and coffee, I make no mistakes. Bob's future might change dramatically if I suggest the wrong course of action. Of course, Dr. Mattia gets the final word. But he rarely disagrees with me. Only occasionally do the ER doctors disagree with me. I hate it when the doctors disagree with my recommendations. My own mental illness just lets loose, and I instantly transform into an 8-year-old boy being reprimanded by my father. He was a doctor, too. Some childhood experiences just never seem to go away.

I have a ten-second window to express myself clearly. "I think he has early stages of organic dementia, possibly Alzheimer's. He needs a nursing home or an assisted care facility, not a mental hospital. A few milligrams of Ativan, and I believe he could go home with a family member. I'll explain to the family their options concerning assisted living, but I'm not sure myself what's available locally."

"Sounds good!"

He's ready to sign before I can even raise my clipboard. If it had been a duel, he would have filled me full of bullet holes. In a flash the window is closed, and he's thinking about another patient or erectile dysfunction, I'm not sure which.

At this point, I'm completely elated because I just got what I wanted; the patient is being discharged, and I don't have to go through the pains of finding him a bed at a mental hospital. I've had to wait as long as fourteen hours to place a patient. Passing by Room 12, I poke my head in to see how my next patient is doing.

"Who the fuck are you?" He leans around the police officer, glaring at me with red swollen eyes.

"My name is Stewart. I'll be back in a few minutes so we can talk."

"Get me the fuck outta here!" His words trail behind me.

I go to the charge nurse CJ, and she smiles. "He's got a lot of energy. You're going to have fun with him."

"It's going to be a long weekend," I reply.

"Are you on through the holiday?"

"All seventy-two hours. I'm off call Monday at five PM."

"What a way to spend Labor Day weekend."

I wink at her. "This keeps me out of trouble, CJ."

What I'm really thinking is a 72-hour shift will keep me sober. Leroy is coming to visit from Florida and Cassandra is off all weekend.

"Dr. Mattia said to discharge Bob in Thirteen," I inform her.

"What's his problem?"

"I think he's having early symptoms of Alzheimer's. He's really scared."

"Poor thing. What about his family?"

"Oh shit! I almost forgot about them."

"They had a pizza delivered."

"To the waiting room?" I'm amazed.

"They're having a real party out there."

"He needs to get away from them and go to an assisted living facility. Do you have any ideas?"

"I do," she replies without hesitation. "I'll make sure they get some information before he leaves."

"He could use a little Ativan to calm his nerves."

She reaches for the key to the drug room and stands up. "How about two milligrams?"

It's not a question. CJ has twice the intellect of most human beings.

"You're a real peach, CJ," I reply as she walks away. I worry for a moment that I was inappropriate. I have obsessive compulsive disorder. It makes you question everything and worry about anything. It can be exhausting.

In the waiting room I find Bob's family laughing about something. I see the empty pizza box sitting in a chair. It crosses my mind that Bob might have money, and if they can get a doctor to diagnose him as incompetent, the family could gain control of his wealth. I've seen the same situation play out many times in the ER, and if that's the case, Bob is going to lose for sure. He's outnumbered. Family doesn't give up easily.

"Where are you going to send him?" They stop laughing and focus on me.

"We are going to release him to you. Bob is showing early signs of dementia, maybe Alzheimer's disease. I can't send him anywhere because he's not actively homicidal or suicidal. That's what the mental hospitals are for."

Bob's family is obviously disappointed with my answer. I continue, "Bob isn't crazy or dangerous. But he will probably need to move into a nursing home of some kind." I'm watching their response closely.

"But he attacked me!"

It's Michael, the son-in-law.

"What were you doing to him?" I reply.

He hesitates. "Trying to get him to the hospital!"

He wrestled a 72-year-old man to the floor. Michael obviously has some built-up resentment toward Bob. I'm instantly tired of the conversation.

"He may not have recognized you," I add.

Maybe it's my tone, but no one says anything else. They reluctantly thank me and slowly march out the door, leaving the cardboard pizza container on the chair. As I'm about to leave, one of Bob's sons comes back in with a question.

"What are the chances I'll have the same problem?"

He appears genuinely concerned. I consider for a moment hitting him about the head with my closed fist. I look down at my pen and wonder how many times I could stab him before security stopped me.

"You're talking genetics, dominant and recessive genes combining, I'm not sure."

"It really scares me." He presses his concern.

I'm feeling no sympathy. "Think how Bob feels," I reply.

I finish my paperwork and go back to the ER to talk to my homicidal patient. It's 1:45 AM, and I'm feeling a little homicidal myself. Dr. Mattia is still commanding the ER from the comfort of his chair. I remember the erectile dysfunction article on his computer screen and accidentally laugh as I walk by. He probably thinks I'm crazy, but it takes mental illness to fully understand mental illness. That's why I'm good at what I do.

My patient is sound asleep in Bed Twelve, and the police officer who's watching him is flirting with the nurses. I'm not comfortable waking patients up. I always worry they will yell at me, and I will transform into that 8-year-old boy being reprimanded by my father once again.

"You will never amount to anything. Get a real job!" I hear the voices.

I go to the officer for some additional information.

"What's his problem?" I get out my handkerchief and rub my glasses.

Sarah hangs up the phone. "We have an overdose coming in ten to fifteen." She looks at me and laughs. It's a nauseating laugh shared by anyone who works in an emergency room. It's not a laugh stimulated by humor, but a laugh that's a defense mechanism to cover up a desire to pull your hair out and scream.

"Business is good!" I say to her. I'd like to get to know Sarah better, but she's separated or going through a divorce, I'm not sure which it is. Because of my job, I have a very low tolerance for personal drama. I keep to myself as much as possible.

The police officer turns to me. "He was in a bar drinking, stood up on a chair, and told everyone he was going to kill them."

I shake my head slowly, trying to remember if I'd ever done the same. "You searched him, right?"

"No weapons."

I glance in the room at the patient. He's in his late fifties with long wild hair and a long-sleeve camo shirt. Sleeping on his side, he has the handcuffs tucked under his head like a pillow.

"He looks like a Vietnam veteran to me," I respond.

"His name is Walter," CJ offers.

"Walter," I repeat his name and go into the room.

The first thing I notice is the smell. It's a combination of body odor and alcohol. You can tell a lot about a patient by the fumes they give off. The smell of a GI bleed is unmistakable. That's blood mixed with feces. Halitosis is the worst. I'm so afraid of having bad breath, I brush and floss three times a day.

Walter is snoring. I put a piece of gum in my mouth.

"Hey, Walter." I turn on the lights. "Walter, wake up. We need to talk." He grunts and stirs a little.

"C'mon, Walter, I have to figure out if you need to go to Oakwood Hospital. Everyone tells me you're homicidal."

Hit hard, hit fast, and be honest. Your honesty will hopefully bring out their honesty. Walter opens his eyes and tries to sit up. I help him by raising the back on the hospital bed. I rarely touch patients unless they insist on a handshake. A good cough can contaminate the air with pinworms for at least twenty seconds.

"You are a disgusting human being, Walter. I wish we had an incinerator here in the ER. I'd personally stuff you into it." The thoughts that go through my mind would scare most people.

Walter appears calm. He might have been homicidal earlier, but he isn't now. I lean against the wall and chew on my gum. Fatigue is getting the best of me. It's late, it's early. I'd like to drink a 6-pack of beer before starting the interview. I could do this job intoxicated. The interviews might improve, but the paperwork would definitely not get done. Walter tries to wipe something out of his eye. The handcuffs rattle. Far from a threat to all his drinking buddies at the bar, now he's submissive. His knees are to his chest, and he's making no eye contact. His head is down, and he appears remorseful.

"I don't need to go to Oakwood Hospital." His voice is low, but clear.

"You ever been there?"

"I go to the VA when I need help."

I look out into the ER to see if the police officer is paying attention. I can see him still flirting with CJ. He's completely forgotten about Walter. The patient could dismember me with a pocketknife before he would have time to respond. I take off my glasses and wipe my eyes, too. I'm pacing the conversation. I want Walter to be comfortable with me, but not too quickly. If I sit in the chair, right away he would lose respect for me. Walter might be acutely mentally ill, but in his mind he's a soldier and always will be. PTSD is permanent. The signs and symptoms can be alleviated, and with enough good therapy sometimes the PTSD can be rendered dormant, but a hand grenade is a hand grenade.

"Did you threaten to kill someone tonight, Walter?"

"Who are you? Are you in the military?" He's instantly upset. So much for me sitting down and relaxing.

"Air Force Academy, '90-91, the first Gulf War," I reply. Walter doesn't need to know the details. I was an assistant coach at the Air Force Academy at the time, a civilian contractor. He grows quiet, only partly understanding the answer.

"I had a bad night, okay? Just get me the fuck out of here, and I will go to the VA hospital in Greensboro. I've been there before."

I'm pleased with his answer. First, he has a solution to his problem of receiving a new charge for communicating threats—he goes to the VA when he becomes psychotic, and second, he thinks I have the power to release him from the ER. I can already sense a disagreement with Dr. Mattia, however:

"But Dr. Mattia, VA hospitals are designed to accept veterans. Our mental hospitals don't like veterans. Plus, the VA won't charge him anything."

My insecurities mount, and my stomach twists in a knot. The coffee and pizza wasn't a good idea. I'm going to have diarrhea for sure. I take a loud deep breath. Walter is wide awake now, listening to the sounds in the ER. My thoughts jump around as I try to formulate the best recommendation for everyone, especially me. It would take the rest of the night on the phone trying to place a veteran in a civilian hospital.

I do the math aloud. "I can probably get you out of here, Walter, but you have to work with me. You can't leave this ER until your blood alcohol level drops well below .08, probably closer to .04, if we're lucky."

Maybe math wasn't his best subject in school, or maybe it is the suggestion he isn't going to leave any time soon, but Walter has a meltdown. In a flash, he kicks the IV tray next to his bed and screams, "Get these fucking handcuffs off me!"

The aluminum tray dances through the air, ricocheting off the wall, then crashes to the floor. The noise is impressive. Walter's cup of water is the only thing on the tray, fortunately. Six ounces of water suddenly looks like ten gallons as it splashes everywhere.

In an instant, CJ appears in the doorway. The police officer is right behind her, looking guilty. Sarah comes around the corner seconds later. Dr. Mattia is in the background making a quick assessment from his chair. I am leaning against the wall, holding my clipboard, casually watching the commotion. I smile at Sarah. She rolls her eyes.

"Yelling in the ER won't help anything, Walter." CJ picks up the tray and replaces it on the stand.

I look past Sarah and see my overdose patient arrive with the fire department paramedics. It's a young girl and both her wrists are bloody.

Sarah leaves and says over her shoulder, "We have a detox on the way."

"What?" I reply.

"Fire Department is bringing in a fifty-year-old male."

I leave the room shaking my head. "Why don't they just go to a detox clinic!"

"Because they like it here!" Sarah's voice gets drowned out by the chaos boiling in the ER.

It's going to be a long Labor Day weekend. I've got my hands full until my shift ends Monday afternoon at 5:00 PM. I look at my watch. It's 2:30 AM, and it's only Saturday morning. On a normal weekend, some nights, I only see two or three patients.

I head for the break room to find another cup of coffee or maybe some more cold pizza. I take a quick inventory of the ER. Beds Twelve, Thirteen, and Trauma Two are mine. The rest, thank God, I can ignore. For now, they are medical emergencies, but that can change.

Acute mental illness can happen to anyone at any time. Part of being human means you have a psychotic core driven by hormones and instincts that can explode instantly if the right conditions present themselves. It's called fight or flight. It's called self-preservation. It's called involuntary manslaughter. The deadly recipe waits for everyone, every day, and every hour.

TWO

I hear a knock on the door, and I open my eyes. The only light in the room is the glow from the LED indicators on all the equipment. I'm lying in a hospital bed in the back of the ER. It's called the Fast Track emergency area. A few beds smaller than the ER, Fast Track accommodates minor injuries and complaints. Typically closed from 11:00 PM to 8:00 AM, here I have a favorite room I sleep in when I get a chance.

It was Sarah knocking on the door. She was gently telling me the sun was almost up and it was time to go home. I had only slept for two hours.

Walter went home with his daughter and promised he would go to the VA medical center as soon as possible. Fortunately, Dr. Mattia agreed to the idea. I called the VA and staffed with one of their doctors. He knew Walter. He gave a vote of confidence that Walter would show up, probably sooner than later. He said Walter comes and goes from the hospital frequently. If he's sober, the PTSD is controllable, but when he starts drinking, he falls apart. Alcohol, the great social lubricant. I simply told Dr. Mattia Walter was going to tear the emergency room to pieces if we restrained him much longer. But that's backwards, right? Release a homicidal patient to his own free will including no handcuffs and police protection? I didn't think twice when Walter proposed the idea. Our veterans don't belong in civilian hospitals.

The girl who tried to kill herself by cutting her wrists and swallowing a handful of painkillers easily survived. It took a few hours of phone work, staffing with receiving nurses and doctors, and faxing reports and forms back and forth. A patient has to be medically cleared before they can be released from the emergency room. Wounds have to be closed, blood has to be diluted with sterile isotonic solution, and drug and alcohol levels have to drop to acceptable limits. Mental hospitals do not like any medical problems. I've staffed with doctors for hours only to have them say, "Sorry, the patient just doesn't meet our admission criteria." I was able to get her transferred to a psychiatric hospital about two hours away. They will probably release her in about ten days, heavily medicated.

The rest of the night was filled with a variety of overdoses and suicidal ideations. Just thinking and talking about suicide rarely gets you a bed in a psychiatric hospital. Real attempts are the way to go.

I sit up and paw at my whiskers. My tongue feels like a five-pound fish in a spoonful of water. I'm listening to the sounds coming from the ER. Sarah kept walking, so I don't have a patient waiting. I look at my watch. It's 7:15 AM.

I tuck my shirt in and grab my briefcase. My goal is to get home, speaking to as few people as possible, but I'll still have to check in at the ER to see if there are any psych patients enroute by ambulance or personal car. Driving while acutely mentally ill isn't difficult.

Shift change is at 1:00 AM for the nurses and doctors. The night crew is long gone. I walk through the Fast Track, enter the ER, and see Dr. Machinski at work shuffling files at the nurses' station. He looks up and nods. Doctors hate paperwork. Everything they do can lead to a lawsuit. Fortunately, he doesn't want to chat about anything. I'm one step closer to the door.

I go to the main hub, and everyone has gathered for an impromptu staff meeting. Someone who calls themselves the Director is giving words of advice about MRSA, a nasty infection that lives on walls and doorknobs. I get a chill just thinking about all the microbes busy colonizing my eyelashes. I see Dr. Mattia is finishing some phone dictation, and Dr. Guda is starting on a new cup of coffee. Dr. Guda always wears loud Hawaiian shirts in the ER. I'm not sure if it's supposed to help relax the patients or him. He's always happy to see me because he hates mental patients.

"Stewart! How goes it?"

"A busy night, Doc. Do you need any information from me?"

He looks around the ER and formulates a summary in two seconds. "Nope," he says with a smile.

I look over his shoulder at one of my patients who came in after nearly drinking himself to death. He got behind the wheel of a car and drove it into a swamp, nearly drowning. He took out a road sign that said "Curve" with the big arrow pointing left or right and apparently tried to fix it. The police said they found him next to the road, after swimming away from the sinking car, trying to pound the sign back in place—a real Samaritan. I guess he didn't want anyone else to miss the curve, too. He passed out shortly after that and didn't wake up.

"What are you going to do with him?" I ask.

"He's got four cracked ribs, a broken arm, and a blood alcohol level of about .4 percent."

"That's impressive," I respond with a nod. Dr. Guda adds a brief chuckle, "Maybe you can talk to him in a few hours."

Let me summarize blood alcohol levels. Medical people refer to percentages, but whole numbers are easier to compare. If you have one drink, you will have a level 2. The legal limit in this state is 8. The Good Samaritan who tried to fix the sign he ran over, who is comatose from alcohol poisoning and a swim in the swamp, came in with a 40, and it was probably higher before we were able to test him. Most people would be dead if they drank that much.

"He'll be admitted because of his injuries, right?" I have no desire to talk to the hooligan. I'm starting to think about having a few drinks myself. After all, my day may have just ended.

"Definitely."

I slap the counter and turn to go. "Call me if you need me, Doc."

"Will do." He's immediately lost in thought.

It's Saturday morning and everything will be quiet for a while. Acute mental illness—homicidal ideations, suicidal ideations and drug and alcohol overdoses—wait until the shadows grow long and the sun sets. I'll be back by five o'clock for sure and maybe sooner if someone has a bad day. My 72-hour on-call tour has barely started.

It's time to see what Leroy is doing.

I make it to my car without further conversation or eye contact with anyone. It's not that I'm afraid to strike up a conversation for fear they might tell me about their mentally ill husband or brother who needs to quit drinking, it's because I've reached my own saturation point. When you help sick people, they bleed on you. Eventually you are so covered in pain and grief it's hard to walk. I stop at my car and wonder if anyone would care if I puked in the parking lot. The seagulls would flock instantly. A stranger would wonder what I was feeding them. Security would reprimand me later. Please don't feed the seagulls in the parking lot. The doctors get pissed when they shit on their cars.

I drive a yellow Jeep. I thought it was cool when I bought it, but now I worry about the color. Look at the yellow Jeep! What's he stand for? Is he queer? Is he non-binary? I have OCD, so I never put the top down. I don't want anyone to recognize me and start an uncomfortable conversation. I look around for witnesses, then quickly get inside.

The sun is climbing over the horizon as I head south along the coastline. Some people think this is paradise, living on the Atlantic Ocean, surrounded by white beaches and clean water. The problem is I can't afford it. Paradise is expensive. I have a realtor who's been looking for over a year, trying to find a home I can afford. A single-wide trailer stuffed into a trailer park with a common access path to a crowded public beach is $350,000. I can't go in debt for thirty years over a trailer.

After twenty minutes of driving, I pull into my parking lot. I see Leroy's pickup truck. Florida plates and a homemade camper shell. It's made out of plywood and two-by-fours. I'm not sure how it stays together in the wind. Maybe it doesn't. I get out of my yellow Jeep and take a quick survey of the parking lot, looking for boards with nails sticking out. It appears safe. I check my phone to make sure my signal is good.

The ER has learned to call my cell phone, bypassing our dispatchers, which is fine with me. They aren't really dispatchers; they are supervisors without names or faces that approve Medicaid dollars.

They pissed off the ER with so many unnecessary financial questions, I just told the nurses to call me directly. When I get to the ER and get the information, I call the Medicaid dispatcher to let them know I'm on the scene with a new patient. You might ask why it's such a screwed-up process, and I would have to say, "Welcome to the world of Medicaid." It's irrational. Government-funded healthcare is like a dog spinning in circles and chasing its tail.

The parking lot is quiet. I get tired of my neighbors asking how my day was. Evidently, my job is much more interesting than most jobs. I live in a condominium on a golf course. Surrounded by other condominiums, my condo backs up to the 10th fairway. Just step out the back door, drop a ball, and you're in play.

That's why Leroy is here. Leroy is practicing for the PGA Senior Tour. I'm not sure how old you have to be to join the Senior Golf Tour, and I doubt Leroy knows either, but I think one of the basic requirements is that you have to be a professional golfer. Leroy makes his own rules. He brought his dog with him, too. I look at the windows on my condominium and notice my blinds are all closed tight. I expect to see my cat pawing for his life against the glass, meowing to get the hell out. Everything looks calm so far.

I go inside, and Leroy wakes up. His dog OB greets me at the door by smelling my crotch. Leroy has taken over the first floor. I can still retreat to the upstairs if things get too crazy. I'm sure my cat is hiding underneath my bed.

"How was work?" Leroy is awake but not willing to get up.

"Everyone is crazy. Business is good." I pat OB once, then kindly push him away. He's determined to smell my crotch again. I stumble against the refrigerator trying to get away. Leroy must be familiar with the sounds of his dog sexually assaulting someone because he yells at OB without looking. He's lying on an air mattress in my living room.

"OB! Get back here!"

I throw the refrigerator door open and search for a beer. Only three remain. Leroy arrived with a case on Thursday night.

"These beers are mine, Leroy." According to current research, a man my height and weight can consume 2.8 drinks and still be within legal limits. It seems a bit liberal to me. As tired as I am, I'll fall down the stairs if I drink three beers.

"Go for it!" I hear the hesitation in his voice.

Ten minutes later we're driving old golf balls across the fairway and into the trees on the other side. The beer tastes good, but I'm not willing to relax. If the ER calls me, I'll need to be there as soon as possible. Occasionally a patient requires sutures or sobering up prior to transport, but delaying my arrival just prolongs my departure.

"I played forty-five holes yesterday," Leroy tells me, warming up with his nine-iron.

"How did you manage that?"

He points left, then right, then sweeps his arm through the air. "I walked ten, eleven, and eighteen five times, playing three balls."

It's a good choice of holes; I've done it before. The triangular path brings you right back to my patio. I immediately worry that the owner of the condominiums, who is also the owner of the golf course, probably watched Leroy do this all day yesterday. I look at OB lying in the grass. Dogs aren't allowed either.

"You never walk, Leroy. How did you carry all your clubs?"

Leroy has the biggest golf bag on the planet. He makes his own clubs and carries about forty or fifty different woods, irons, and hybrids no one has ever seen before.

"Well, I took just three clubs and focused on improving my swing."

Again, I think of Eddie, the owner, sitting on the porch of the clubhouse with his feet on the railing, smoking a cigar, wondering who the hell Leroy belongs to. Holes ten and eighteen both go right by the clubhouse. I notice Leroy's travel cooler airing out next to the grill. A beer per hole is his standard recipe.

"Hold up a minute. There's a guy coming down the fairway." I go inside to find another beer. I may not get any sleep, but I'm definitely getting a shower. I can catch up on sleep Monday night after my shift is over. Maintaining a positive attitude is paramount when a working crisis calls. As long as you're eating well, hydrating properly, and smiling, you can deal with the drama. If you let your own mental health slip, maybe because you just had an argument with a state trooper, then you won't survive. Counseling acutely mentally ill patients requires a clear mind. Otherwise, it would be comparable to using a dirty needle on a patient. Doctors try to use clean needles.

"I saw a guy last night who was so drunk, he took out a road sign and drove into a swamp. He had to swim back to the road."

"What did the sign say?"

"'Curve.'"

Leroy laughs heartily. I'm sure he's done the same thing before. I've had similar experiences, but never ended up in an emergency room.

"I need to get a shower, Leroy. It's a holiday weekend. I don't suspect the ER will be quiet for long."

"Where's the nearest Trade Mart?" he replies.

"You drove right by one getting here."

Leroy is the only person I know who drinks Milwaukee's Best beer. And not just drinks it—he lives on it. The company should hire Leroy and conduct tests, watching for tumors and unsightly appendages. Trade Mart sells Milwaukee's Best for about ten dollars a case. Before I know it, he's gone, with OB hanging out the window and slobbering down the side of the pickup truck. It's good to have Leroy around. As long as he has a beer in one hand and a golf club in the other, he's the happiest person in the world to spend time with. Emerson once said, "Simplify, simplify, simplify." Leroy is a master of simplicity, but if I get the chance, I'm going to ask him if he wants me to send him to a detox facility.

I shower, then fall asleep as quickly as I can. I'm hoping for a quiet two-hour nap to purge my mind, and sure enough at 11:00 AM my phone rings.

"This is Bonnie calling from the emergency room. Dr. Bowry would like to speak to you."

"Sure. Sure, put him on." There's a long pause. Dr. Bowry is probably juggling three phone conversations at the same time. Always an optimist, I think Dr. Bowry enjoys the drama of the ER more than the other doctors. The worse things get, the more he focuses. I always get more calls when he's on duty because he knows I'm the same way.

"This is Dr. Bowry."

"Hey, Doc, this is Stewart. What can I help you with?"

"I've got an eighteen-year-old male patient who says he's suicidal. I think we could send him home, but I wanted a second opinion."

"No problem. I'll be there in about forty-five minutes."

I hang up and look at the empty beer can next to my bed. Dr. Bowry has no idea I spent the night at the ER. The doctors only work 8-hour shifts. They just assume we work reasonable hours, too. Suddenly my 72-hour shift feels like it will never end.

A few minutes later, as I'm about to get in my yellow Jeep, Cassandra pulls into the parking lot and parks next to me. She rolls down her window and loud music pours across the pavement.

"The bloody traffic sucks around here. A bunch of limeys have arrived from Raleigh." She turns down the music. It's a British punk band no one around here has ever heard. I shake my head and laugh. The momentary distraction is good. Suddenly I'm not thinking about how I can help a suicidal patient.

Cassandra was born and raised in London. She served with the British Army and once handed a tiger cub to Princess Diana, as part of a military celebration. I asked her what she did with the tiger. "Quickly passed it on!" was her answer.

I look in the backseat of her worn BMW and see three mannequins sitting in various positions, looking in different directions out the windows. With their pale expressionless faces and fancy attire, it would be hard to let Cassandra drive by without a second glance.

"I see you are car-pooling to work today."

"A half-day. I'm ready for a drink already. After I get rid of these models, I'll be done for the weekend."

"Where are they going?" I lean over and look in the window. She could have just as easily put them in the trunk to avoid shocking someone.

"A department store."

"Well, have fun. I wish I could play with dolls. I'm off to talk to someone who is suicidal."

"Just tell them to off themselves." She turns up the music.

"Come back later. Leroy is here. I'll be in and out all weekend."

Cassandra is good at entertaining herself. She's very independent. Even if I don't show up all night, she and Leroy will have fun drinking Milwaukee's Best and talking trash. I drive back to the ER with a lump in my throat and a knot in my stomach. Meanwhile, Leroy is out enjoying his private utopia of cold beer and free golf.

THREE

"Don't make me drive two hours to get my paycheck. You'll be sorry if I have to drive ninety miles just to get paid!"

I hang up the phone and look around to see if anyone heard me. I just communicated a threat to my boss. It's a misdemeanor if she recorded the conversation. No one else is in the admissions department where I'm reviewing patient charts, so I convince myself it's okay. Anyhow, they shouldn't be surprised by my rude behavior. It's been three weeks since I saw a paycheck, and we're supposed to get paid every two weeks. That's three weeks of overdue pay. Thankfully I'm not living paycheck to paycheck, at least for now.

Our society assumes if you suffer an acute psychological breakdown, qualified and supportive medical personnel will come to your rescue. Well, it's not true. If you call 911, you will probably get a fireman who has basic emergency training. He or she might be a volunteer. If someone more qualified shows up, consider yourself lucky. If that's the case, you probably live in a metropolitan area with a hospital close by. The rest of the country flies by the seat of its pants.

My paycheck is three weeks late because the company that won the contract isn't qualified to manage crisis calls. They're just people with bachelor's degrees in social work or business who convinced a doctor to sign off on all the billing. It's called Medicaid fraud, and it happens every day, in every state, all across America. It's no wonder Medicaid is going bankrupt.

The people I work for don't have a clue how to do my job. There's no formal training, and there aren't any classes. I learned from being a paramedic and watching a handful of other counselors, who are all long gone. Burnout is fast. The average crisis counselor career lasts six months. The only requirement is that you can communicate with crazy people. Having some intelligence helps too. The only worthwhile research I ever read on the subject summarized two goals when working with homicidal and suicidal patients: identify the patient's strengths and create future orientation. All that means is, try to find something the patient is good at doing, then convince them they can do it tomorrow if they can keep their shit together. I never stray far from meeting those two goals.

I already staffed with Dr. Bowry about the patient. For now, he's my only patient and the ER is quiet. A three-day weekend, and he's the first casualty. I'm reading his chart to figure out what happened. His name is Timothy and he's 18 years old. Everyone hates to see young people in distress, but it's not unusual for a teenager to show up at the ER, usually after tearing the house apart. Spanking isn't a good solution for a homicidal/suicidal meltdown.

I'm not familiar with the weekend day shift. Nobody knows me either. The chemistry between ER staff is paramount. The right combination of people can handle any amount of chaos, whereas one wrong personality injected into the mix can create distress for everyone, including the patients. I'm hoping that Sarah and CJ are working tonight.

"What's your major malfunction today, Timothy?" I ask aloud. I'm sitting in my favorite cubicle in the admission area. The admission staff filters the insanity that pours into the ER. Located between the waiting room and the ER, it's an area filled with telephones, computer screens, copiers, and fax machines. A persistent aroma of coffee and popcorn wafts through the illness. Shelly is on duty until midnight—thank goodness for a familiar face. Shelly went to a Rascal Flats concert last night, and I don't think anything could put her in a bad mood.

"What are you listening to?" I ask.

She removes an earbud with both feet tapping the floor.

"Rascal Flats!"

"I thought they broke up?"

Like many employees at a hospital, Shelly is juggling her 40-hour-a-week job with school. I think she's taking nursing classes.

"Looks like Timothy is back," she whispers.

A mental breakdown demands a good investigation. I've learned to pick everyone's brain for information, especially if the patient is lying or trying to hide something. Typically, a psychotic patient will spill their guts to the admit staff, quickly turn paranoid, then clam up when they see all the lab coats and needles in the ER.

"Who brought Timothy in?" I inquire.

"His grandmother. She's in the family room."

"Ah, the family room. I love the family room."

"You wanna see his visitation record?"

Shelly's fingers dance on the keyboard and a huge record scrolls down the screen.

"Holy shit," I reply, looking over her shoulder. "Does he get mail here?"

"We're too nice to him," she summarizes.

"Maybe I can send him to Oakwood Hospital. He won't like that."

"You probably need to send his grandmother, too."

More coded conversation. Shelly was mixing fact with some opinion, but working the front line as she does, her exposure to the patient's original presentation and demeanor is priceless. What she was saying to me was that the whole family is mentally ill, and Timothy is their point man. He's just the manifestation of a deeper sickness. There's probably something heinous going on at home.

I have a choice between seeing the patient first or going to the family room. Both conversations are important; which one comes first is always a guess. I've talked to Timothy before, so I decide to interview the grandmother to learn something new. Sometimes the family is delusional, folie à deux or madness for two. Families can exacerbate and manifest mental illness easily. They share it for breakfast and drive one another crazy all day long. Everyone eats prescription medication like candy and the alcohol is plentiful. And parents always wonder why their kids are so screwed up. "It's because you taught them to be mentally ill, you idiots!"

I've heard theories about how retardation can be a by-product of the environment. In other words, a child can turn into a moron simply because proper stimulation didn't exist. I saw a patient regularly who was diagnosed with mild mental retardation. He spent most of his infancy in a soiled diaper, strapped in a baby car seat while his mother smoked cocaine. He had a measured IQ of about 50. Not surprisingly, he was also diagnosed with bipolar disorder and spent a lot of time locked up in mental hospitals.

"Hello, I'm Stewart with the crisis team. Dr. Bowry wanted me to talk to Timothy. Maybe you can tell me what's going on?"

I just hit the ball into Grandma's court. I didn't even give her a chance to introduce herself. Introductions don't matter much.

She blinks a few times and moves to the edge of her seat. Her hands start moving first, then her arms as she tries to formulate a logical response. Everyone that shows up at an emergency room is guilty of something. An emergency room is a harbor for chaos. It's a respite for dysfunctional behavior. Everyone that visits has screwed up terribly, whether it's due to an unhealthy lifestyle, inheriting flawed genes, or driving left of center. No one shows up because they are having a good day. It's human behavior at its worst.

"Well, he isn't taking his medication," she starts.

Now that's a surprise.

"Did you take out the IVC papers on Timothy?"

"Yes. I told the magistrate he was going to kill someone."

I take a jagged breath and sit down. It's a sore issue with me. IVC: involuntary commitment. Just think about it for a moment. You can be committed involuntarily to any emergency room at any time and in any place. All it takes is a convincing story and a magistrate's signature. A magistrate is a judge who handles last-minute, after-hours emergency decisions.

"Did he try to kill you?"

She's not sure.

Involuntary commitment is available in every county, in every courthouse, across the nation, twenty-four hours a day, seven days a week. And if not at the courthouse, a magistrate is always on call waiting to respond to a court emergency. Magistrates work with local police departments to set bail and send people to jail. Magistrates can marry people. Magistrates can sign orders for arrest. Magistrates can release people from jail. And, magistrates can send people to the emergency room, against their will, to be evaluated for suicidal or homicidal ideations if the concerned party is sober enough to paint a suspicious picture of the victim. I say victim because when a family member takes out an IVC on another family member, the story is usually filled with bullshit. It's simply not true. But the magistrate has to cover his ass, and the ER has to cover its ass.

"He's just not right. He's out of his head."

I look at the clock on the wall. Leroy is probably putting right now, trying not to hit the beer can sitting on the green. Leroy likes to drink two or three beers at once but will finish none of them. The next morning it's not unusual to find a 12-pack of opened beers half-finished everywhere. You'd think there was a huge party, but it's just Leroy. I don't think his memory is very good.

"It's one o'clock in the afternoon," I say out loud.

Grandma gathers her senses and looks at me bewildered.

"Do you like golf?"

I'm testing her orientation. Seeing if she can carry two conversations at once. What the hell. She's probably not going to say anything interesting. We've talked many times before.

"My husband used to play."

"That's Timothy's grandfather?"

"He's dead."

"How did he die?"

"Cancer."

"Was he good at golf?"

"Yes."

"Does Timothy get angry when he plays golf?"

It's a stupid question. I'm having trouble following my own reasoning.

"Well, he did when he was little."

She thinks the information is relevant. Maybe it is.

"But he stopped playing when he got older."

"How much older?"

"I'm not sure. Maybe when he turned eighteen."

I look at the chart.

"He's eighteen now."

She pauses. "Yes."

Grandma is alert but not oriented. Which means her interpretation of "going to kill someone" is questionable. Timothy has problems for sure, but he may not need to be locked up in a mental hospital today. And he may not be homicidal. Suddenly the conversation about golf is relevant. I think it's called serendipity, something for free. Rare for sure.

"I'll see what I can do." And I leave Grandma in the family room to read the latest issue of *People* magazine.

The family room has two doors; one goes to the waiting room and the other directly to the ER. I punch the numbers on the keypad and step onto my stage. Everyone notices me for a split second, then goes back to being busy. The staff wants Timothy to leave as soon as possible, not because they don't care, but because a bus full of children on a field trip could collide with a freight train at any time. Emergency rooms run on adrenaline and paranoia.

Dr. Lowder is absent so he must be with a patient. Trauma and sickness outweigh mental illness probably five to one, so emergency room staff think mentally ill patients are a waste of time. They aren't supposed to be in the emergency room. They are supposed to be in another part of the hospital that doesn't exist in small county hospitals. Psychiatrists work in large urban hospitals, big hospitals with big emergency rooms and heliports on the roof. Small hospitals can't afford psychiatrists or psychiatric units. So, if you are suicidal and you want help, get in line, a long line.

I cross through the ER to Timothy's room, stopping for a moment to staff with the charge nurse, then the attending nurse, in that order. ER staff are highly territorial. Like I said, it's Saturday afternoon, so I'm not familiar with the crew. I think the charge nurse is overly caffeinated. Probably too much coffee or Mountain Dew.

"Hello. I'm Stewart with the Crisis Team."

"He's all yours. Mary is his nurse."

She quickly points to Mary, and the conversation is over. Mary is in a hurry, trying to keep up with six patients and sixty orders. I watch her disappear into a room. I stand still, trying not to be drawn in by the chaos. The atmosphere in an emergency room can be toxic. I suddenly feel strange. I'm not sure if I'm standing or sitting. My clipboard weighs fifty pounds. I feel hot and surrounded by bright light. I think I'm going to soil myself. I look up.

"God, I didn't know we had so many skylights in here." The ceiling is covered with skylights and sunshine is streaming in everywhere.

The charge nurse realizes I'm still standing next to her. She holds the phone away from her head and stops dialing.

"You guys work mostly nights, don't you?"

I'm still looking at the skylights. I start to wonder about security issues and surveillance satellites.

"I always work nights, but this time I'm working all weekend. I go off call Monday afternoon at five PM."

It's a fraternity. She can read my mind. She can see me driving home at five o'clock Monday, drinking a beer from a paper bag, so acutely mentally ill that I can't wait to get home to marinate myself until I pass out. She smiles.

"I wouldn't do your job if they doubled my pay."

The receptionist next to her nods her head in agreement.

I laugh. I know I'm always just one step away from being a patient, handing my clipboard over to someone else.

"I especially like schizophrenics. They're fun to talk to," I reply.

"Well, you'll have to wait because Timothy is just crazy."

Mary appears from a room with a used syringe and joins the conversation. She evidently has good hearing.

"Hi, Mary. I'm Stewart from the Crisis Team."

She knows the drill.

"Timothy is manic today," she says, dropping the bloody syringe into a container.

"Has he been taking his meds?" I ask.

She hands me the lab analysis. I taught myself how to read the blood and urine lab reports. Over time, if you ask the right questions, you figure out what's normal and what's not. Most of the ER staff think we went to school for this stuff.

"He's not taking his lithium," I conclude.

I got lucky. It was an easy diagnosis. Lithium naturally occurs in your body; it's created naturally. If your levels are low, you might have issues. Normal is 0.5 to 1.2 milligrams per some unit like deciliters. Timothy has a 0.2. However, that was a medical diagnosis, not a psychological evaluation. Lithium levels may not be Timothy's problem, but the numbers make everyone feel better.

The unspoken fraternal order again. Everyone nods their head in unison, convinced the numbers never lie. Western medicine relies on numbers, not faith, intuition, and feelings. All the numbers do is create more lab tests and further evaluation.

"Well, let's see if his grandma gets her wish to send him to Oakwood Hospital today, and get him out of the house for a while," I summarize.

The ten-second conversation is over. I look at my clipboard to hide my thoughts. I still feel like soiling myself. My stomach begins to boil and make noise. Damnit, I think. I've got some food poisoning. It might have been the cold pizza, maybe Leroy's cheap beer, maybe the cafeteria food. I excuse myself to my favorite bathroom in the back of the Fast Track area, past my favorite hospital bed. I look in to make sure there isn't a patient dying or bleeding everywhere. The room is empty. I can sleep here again tonight if I have to. I always wonder who used the bed last when I sleep in it.

Back in the ER I go to Timothy's room. Dr. Lowder is in the command center, in his favorite chair, juggling ten patients; so far, I just have one. He's parked in front of the computer, entering notes and dictating on the phone. Everything gets recorded here. He sees me and nods his head.

If Superman was short and weighed about 150 pounds, Dr. Lowder could fill his shoes. He's the ultimate adrenaline junkie and was probably playing with a stethoscope instead of a pacifier when he was a baby. I've never seen him tired. He appears to love his work, although it could be just an act. I knew an emergency room doctor that gave up his career to be a carpenter. I worked with him. He didn't show any signs of burnout. Then he was gone. That could be me anytime. Fortunately, thoughts are still invisible here. If someone could read my mind, I'd have to kill them.

But here's the funny part about Dr. Lowder: his brother Brian works in this ER, too, as an emergency room doctor. Dr. Brian Lowder is also an ER physician. What are the chances of that happening? Two brothers both end up working as ER physicians in the same ER. They don't look at all alike, and I've never noticed any real comradery between them. Doctors choose to train as ER physicians in medical school. There was a time when any MD could work in an emergency room, but specialization has mostly eliminated the general practitioner, GP-MD, who was once willing and crazy enough to do such a thing.

I enter Timothy's room and we're alone for the moment. The staff is good about not interrupting my patient interviews. It's understood that most people don't like to air out their dirty laundry to a crowd, unless you're bipolar and cycling through a manic phase.

"Timothy, good to see you."

He misses the humor and wants to shake my hand.

"Dr. Stewart, how are you?"

He's the last person I want to touch right now, so I lean toward him and whisper, "I've got a bad case of diarrhea. You don't want to shake my hand if you know what I mean."

The information is true, but I'm also trying to eliminate any communication barrier that might be present. If I bare my soul, and share my secrets, he likely will too. Timothy has problems, but his family is mentally ill as well.

He quickly pulls his hand back and reaches for his drink which is next to his warm lunch. Food is plentiful in an ER.

"Why aren't you taking your lithium?"

"I don't need it."

"You might be right, Timothy."

Bipolar patients in a manic cycle never want medication. I've heard them say, "It just feels too good to be so high. Why would I want to come down?"

"Your grandmother says you've been acting manic at home. What's been going on?"

"I was just playing around with a baseball bat. I wouldn't give it to her."

"Are you sure it wasn't a golf club?"

"I was swinging the bat in the kitchen and accidentally hit the refrigerator."

That's easy to imagine. I guess I could do the same. I'm thinking with my pen scribbling on my clipboard now. I was putting on the carpet with Leroy last night. That's similar.

"Were you trying to hurt anyone?"

"No, Dr. Stewart, but I think my family is trying to hurt me."

Suicidal ideations are negative. Homicidal ideations are negative. I stop writing.

"Why?"

"My dad sexually assaulted me."

"When?"

"Recently."

"What do you mean by sexual assault, Timothy?"

"He tried to rape me."

Timothy presses against the hospital bed and squirms as if it took some effort to share the information. He appears authentic. It's a common tactic to distract the interviewer in hopes that you won't be sent to a psychiatric hospital for two weeks. But this is different. Even if it's true that his father tried to rape him, it wouldn't change the accusation by the grandmother who initiated the IVC proceedings. Timothy is being evaluated at the ER because a reliable friend or family member or professional observed he was a danger to himself and others. Furthermore, I know that Timothy lives with lots of family members in a very dysfunctional home.

I put my pen in my shirt pocket and push my glasses up my nose.

"That sucks, Timothy. I'm sorry to hear that happened to you. Has this ever happened before?"

Now I'm letting him feel accepted. I'm giving merit to his story and hiding any trace of doubt I might have. I want to know if he can provide meaningful details. If not, he might be delusional or maybe it was just a bad dream he transferred into his reality.

"He used to rape me when I was younger, but it hasn't happened in a long time."

I stand up. "I'll see what I can do, Timothy. I'll talk to Dr. Lowder." With that I leave.

Timothy looks strangely relieved. Truth or fiction, at this point it doesn't matter. The patient is not suicidal or homicidal. He might be manic but is not deserving of a trip to a mental hospital, and more pressing, the patient just told a medical caregiver he had been sexually assaulted, which needs to be reported to law enforcement. It's the law. Fortunately, the sheriff deputy who brought Timothy in with his IVC papers is flirting with the nurses and staying close to Timothy's room.

I walk to the counter and silently join the conversation, shuffling some of my papers on my clipboard. Mary looks up at me and waits for my summary. I notice Dr. Lowder is enjoying a Diet Coke while signing orders, talking on the phone, and reading Headline News on his computer. Maybe it's caffeine that keeps him going. I'm wondering if I can speed home after this and drink a few beers with Leroy.

"You're going to love this," I say. Everyone focuses on me. I'm relishing the authority. "Timothy said he was raped by his father, like within the past week."

Everybody drops their head as if the information had too much weight. "The good news is he's not suicidal or homicidal, so we can send him home after the good officer here takes a report."

"He'll be back."

"Of course."

"What about Grandmother?"

"Oh God," I blurt out. It's also part of my job to rid the ER of family members, but Timothy's grandmother had escaped my mind for a moment.

"Does anyone else want to talk to her?" I inquire.

"And ask why her son is a freak?"

I just smile.

"I'll talk to Dr. Lowder." And I'm done reporting to his nurse.

Dr. Lowder gladly invites me into his private Idaho.

"Stewart, how is Timothy?" He already knows, but I'm betting he doesn't know anything about the sexual assault.

"No suicidal ideations. No homicidal ideations. But he did tell me his dad recently sexually assaulted him. The sheriff's deputy is going to take a report. I'm trying to figure out what to say to Grandma."

"What about the baseball bat in the kitchen?"

I pause. "Well, I was swinging a five-iron in my living room last night and no one got hurt."

He offers a short laugh. It's the fraternity again. We're all members here. My report was to the point and left no opening for discussion. Sure, Timothy was swinging a bat in the kitchen, maybe out of anger, but deep down we all empathize. Timothy is mentally ill because his family is mentally ill. Apparently at least three generations deep.

"So IVC is terminated?"

"Yes, sir."

He's happy now. One less patient in his ER. I leave him to juggle lab results and x-rays. I go to the family room to talk to Grandma. Family is usually disappointed when the sick family member gets released and returns to the hive.

FOUR

I speed home in my yellow Jeep, knowing the ER won't be quiet for long. The sun is out and it's warm, but my top is up. I thought I would enjoy a convertible, but the environmental exposure is too intense. The bugs. The fumes. You can hear conversations while waiting for red lights. I get enough of humanity as a crisis counselor.

Dr. Lowder laughed when he saw me leaving the ER. "Sure you don't want to stick around? I'm sure I can find you some business."

"Thanks, Doc. Call me if you need me. I'm right around the corner." And I nearly ran out the door.

Time management is crucial when you are on call for seventy-two hours. It's possible I won't get any sleep for the next forty-eight hours. My short-term goal is a cold beer and some mindless bantering with Leroy.

When I arrive at the golf course and pull into the parking lot, I notice my front door is open. Then I see Leroy's pickup truck with clothes spread across the hood and hanging over the tailgate. OB is lying behind the truck, more or less in the way of traffic. OB is short for out of bounds. I call him OD sometimes, like an overdose. I steer around OB and park. My cat probably ran away. I'm sure Leroy forgot I even had one. OB gets up and tries to smell my crotch, but I sidestep him and hurry inside. The back door is wide open too, and the AC is running hard trying to keep up.

I open the refrigerator, hoping it is stocked with beer and food. I see an 18-pack of Milwaukee's Best. I shake the box and count ten beers. Next to the beer, three cans of tuna, but not for my cat. Leroy is minimalist. He doesn't like complications, and he doesn't embrace technology or modern conveniences very much. His life is simple and inexpensive. His close friends agree he could start a religious commune and be very successful. It would be one of the places you hear about in the news where everyone wears robes and no underwear, and all the women have to take turns sleeping with Leroy. He eats tuna right out of the can and drinks beer most days. Add to that a rigorous golf schedule and he's surprisingly healthy.

"Hey, Leroy!" I'm still staring into the refrigerator and hoping a frozen pizza will magically appear. OB walks into the kitchen and yawns.

I grab a beer and put my briefcase on the counter next to three handmade golf clubs, a pair of golf shoes, and more laundry. I'm fighting my OCD, thinking that I should vacuum and dust everything. My clean and quiet condo on the golf course has turned into a locker room. It's round one of the Senior Tour and the tournament is all in Leroy's head.

I go to the patio and leave the doors open. Airing out Leroy's locker room is probably a good idea. I stand in the sun for a moment and guzzle the beer. Leroy is working on his short game. He's organized a miniature nine-hole challenge using beer cans and a pitching wedge.

"Are those full or empty?"

"They were full." He doesn't take his eye off the ball. His nerves are coated with Milwaukee's Best aluminum. The ball knocks over a can.

"What's that bright ball of light in the sky?" I ask, finishing my beer.

The club reflects sunbeams, and another can falls victim. Leroy screams as if he won the tournament. I quickly scan the windows to the other condos to see who's watching or calling the police. Everyone is hiding, it seems.

"Are you still on call?" We're both looking across the fairway. Not many people are playing. Not many ever do. The course isn't very well maintained. I think it's just a tax shelter for Eddie. Locals that know Eddie say he went from middle class to upper class overnight. "He was just one of us," someone told me. "Then one day he had millions." People tell me things I don't want to hear.

I look at Leroy. I shove my phone in his face. "I'm waiting for the devil to call."

He smiles. "They pay you to get tortured like this?"

"Usually. Although I think I'm volunteering right now."

OB comes out to join us.

"Have you seen my cat?"

"I think he's upstairs."

My cat's name is Scar. He's cool as far as cats go. He's probably happy because I don't let him go upstairs. Now he's lying on my bed licking his butt.

"Have you met Rick yet?" Rick lives in the condo next door. He shares Leroy's dream of joining the Senior Tour. Seems it's an epidemic. I stare into my empty beer can.

"We're going to play tomorrow morning. What does it cost to play eighteen holes with a cart?"

I laugh and walk away to get another beer. "I have no idea, Leroy. I always carry my clubs, and it's free for me!"

He finds that to be funny and he laughs back. "Fuck you!" he calls out.

Mindless bantering is healthy. Humans are herd animals. We want to connect with one another, especially on simple and relaxed levels. That's why we tolerate waiting for red lights and eating together in crowded restaurants.

The phone rings, but it's not the ER. It's my home phone. It's Cassandra. She's driving through Jacksonville, shocking people with her mannequins. I'm surprised the police never pull her over.

"The traffic is bloody awful. I'm surrounded by angry people."

"Leroy and I are drinking beers. C'mon over and visit."

"Splendid idea."

She may or may not stop by. Cassandra is a free spirit. People like that never stay in one place for long. I'm no different. I get nervous if someone recognizes me in a public place like a grocery store. They usually want to tell me about a relative who drinks too much. I've had lots of conversations about IVCs while perusing the beer cooler at the gas station.

"Just go to the local magistrate with a good story. It's really easy," I usually tell them.

The toilet flushes and I wonder what it was I ate. It could've been anything in the break room: cold pizza, warm pizza, doughnuts. Fruits and vegetables aren't part of my diet anymore. I only eat well when I'm not working and I'm relaxing at home. I break into a cold sweat, thinking I might have contracted a virus from one of the patients I interviewed.

❃ ❃ ❃

I had to leave Leroy at home by himself; Cassandra was on her way over when I got a call from the ER. OB was asleep on my leather couch and Scar is missing. Back in the chart room, I try to collect my thoughts. I take a deep breath. My stomach is starting to boil. I can feel it gurgling and bubbling. It's just as well I got called back to the ER. At least I've sobered up. Maybe Cassandra will enjoy Leroy's company and babysit him until he passes out.

The fluorescent lights are bothering me. I turn them off and adjust a table lamp. The chart room is a peaceful place. I'm hidden and alone for the moment. The staff knows I'm here. The chaos is only a few walls away, and they usually leave me alone to study the patient before talking to the patient. Sometimes I'll get an offer for a cup of coffee, and occasionally the ER physician will come in to discuss a patient or hope to get a good laugh from someone. Sarcasm is a great social lubricant. I use it frequently.

I dial Shelly in the other room, hoping to get a forecast of the night ahead. She usually has an accurate prediction of whether the ER will be calm or all hell is going to break loose. She's not answering. I can hear Rascal Flat**s** through the wall. I'll catch her when I'm finished with the patient chart. So far it looks like a regular substance abuse problem. Someone has a monkey on their back, but times two. Both the husband and wife have checked themselves in.

"Hi, Robert. I'm Stewart. Dr. Mattia wanted me to talk to you."

He doesn't correct me to tell me his name is Bob or that friends call him Bobby. He wants a formal conversation. He's here to make a permanent lifestyle change, at least in his mind, and he wants help doing it.

"You are here with your wife, right?"

He shakes his head and fights back his emotions. My butt puckers and I fight back another bowel movement. I've got a bad case of food poisoning, and it's going to kick my ass before it's over. It was probably cold pizza in the break room or at home. It's all I eat when I'm on call, comfort food. I need to drink a lot of beer the first chance I get. That will counter the invasion of microbes for sure. I cross my legs and look at my watch. I've got forty-eight hours left on my shift.

"Our son killed himself three months ago."

Now that's interesting. Thanks for the wake-up call, Robert. I forget about my diarrhea for the moment.

"How did he kill himself?" I'm allowed to ask questions like that.

"Drug overdose. He had some prescriptions and was drinking. My wife and I have been drinking since it happened. But anyone would drink too much if their son had died, for God's sake! I just want to drink less. I'll just moderate from now on."

I look at Robert closely. He has a black eye. Aside from that he looks like the kind of man familiar with a steady income and a home. He looks well nourished and responsible. I look at the chart; he's 47. His blood alcohol level was .341 when tested. Again, .08 is the legal limit for operating a motorized vehicle.

"How did you get the black eye?"

"I fell against the bedpost."

I hold back laughter. I've heard this excuse before. It's either a common lie or a class action lawsuit waiting to hit headline news: Beds Are Dangerous - Call Your Lawyer. I've never had this problem. Maybe passing out on the couch is safer. I think of OB lying on my couch and scratching for fleas.

"How much do you drink?"

"I drink every day. I drink a fifth of vodka and a handful of beers most days."

I look at his hands.

"How many is a handful?"

"About a six-pack."

Beer versus liquor: beer has more nutritional value, more carbohydrates and some protein. It says so right on the can. Liquor is distilled. It's been somewhat purified. A beer drinker doesn't need to eat much. Look at Leroy. Aside from his beer, he drinks coffee in the morning and eats a few cans of tuna the rest of his waking hours. Leroy likes to say beer has food value; food doesn't have beer value. A liquor drinker tends to need more food. If you want to lose your beer belly, switch to vodka.

"Are you eating, Robert?"

"Sometimes. Look, I'll be fine. I just want to go home now. This was my wife's idea."

"I'll talk to Dr. Mattia. I'll see what I can do." I get up to leave. I look at his face one more time. I look into his eyes to see what his intentions are. He's self-absorbed. He just wants to go home and pickle himself again. Alcohol starts out as a friend, then becomes your lover. I exit the room and head straight for the bathroom.

❀ ❀ ❀

"I'm Stewart. Dr. Mattia wants my recommendation. I've already talked to your husband."

I eliminated her smoke screen. There's no room for lies or deceit. People come to ERs for different reasons, many of them dishonest. Some fake suicidal ideations to get out of jail or work or away from abusive spouses. For all I know, she gave him the black eye, and both are seeking painkillers from Dr. Mattia. I put a piece of gum in my mouth. I'm starting to feel dehydrated. It's only 7:00 PM. I could call another counselor in to replace me but that's like asking another soldier to replace you on the front line. You just don't do it. Plus, it's only severe diarrhea. At least I'm not vomiting.

I sit heavily in the chair and look at her closely for any bruising about the arms and neck. She appears well kempt and nourished like her husband. There isn't any evidence she was in a physical fight with him. Maybe he did fall against the bedpost. She seems to be in the mood to talk.

"It was my idea to come here. I was concerned about my husband. I drink vodka every evening until I pass out. I sleep all day and start drinking again when I wake up. I know I have a problem. I'm surprised I could fall to such a low level of existence." She looks me straight in the eye to make sure I'm listening. "I'm a nurse. I worked here locally until a few months ago."

She knows the routine. She knows the language spoken here. I take a deep breath and quietly sigh some relief. There's nothing I need to say. I just wait for her to continue.

"I don't want to die, if that's what you are thinking?"

I'm temporarily at a loss for words. I'm usually the one asking the sensitive questions.

"No. I believe you." I pause and take off my glasses, rubbing my eyes. My guard is down now. "It's just that alcohol is extremely addicting," I add. "You might need some help sobering up. I'll make some calls and see if any of the local detox facilities have beds available. Some of these places are pretty nice. A week, maybe ten days, you will be ready to face your pain…sober."

She looks at me again as if this is the first real conversation she's had in a long time. I feel vulnerable and weak. I turn to my clipboard and write something nonsensical. I stand up to go.

"Thank you, Dr. Stewart." She puts out her hand.

Most people that come to an ER for help are in denial of some kind. My main objective is always to break down the lies and self-deception, to get to the truth behind their motives. These are suicidal and homicidal people. They want to kill themselves. They want to kill others, then kill themselves.

I cross the ER and go to Dr. Mattia. He's interested in getting two patients out at once. Two less problems to worry about. Two beds back to available status. It's just simple math to an ER physician. Sarah takes notice of my pale complexion and sunken eyes and looks concerned.

"You ever hit your face on a bedpost?" I ask Dr. Mattia.

"I'm not buying it," he replies.

Dr. Mattia has a different perspective. He needs to be suspicious. He has the final word, after all. He can sign away life and death. Apparently, he doesn't want to send them home. Finding a mental hospital interested in a husband and wife that drink too much is going to be difficult. Only a psychiatrist wanting to fill some empty beds to meet a quota would accept such nonsense. The system is saturated. The mental health system tries to ignore people like this. Just send them home and wait for one of them to try to kill themselves. Wait for a real suicide attempt. Insurance might pay for that.

"I'll see if I can find a bed, or two beds, at a detox facility. Maybe they would go voluntarily."

I leave him with that thought. What I really wanted to say was, "Hey, Doc, these people are screwed up, but they still have some time before they hit bottom."

The ER doctors only partially understand my job. Finding a mental hospital for someone who doesn't have deep cuts in their wrists or a stomach full of pills is an all-night process. I'll be on the phone for hours. Again, all the beds at all the mental hospitals and detox facilities are full, and the waiting list is days long and growing. If you want help with substance abuse or suicidal ideations, take a deep breath and get in line.

I go to Sarah to give her an update. She's got her hands full as the ER is showing signs of a busy night ahead. One of the nurses is screening an EMS call from an incoming ambulance. Dr. Guda is trying to finish and go home. I see Shelly march in and out with three new charts and three new admissions.

"You look like shit. What's wrong?" Sarah inquires.

"Leroy gave me an STD."

"How's old Leroy doing?"

Sarah has never met Leroy, but she knew he was visiting this weekend. "He's at home playing golf in the dark and drinking all my beer. I'm sure all my windows and doors are wide open."

"Poor Scar!"

The girl has a memory that won't quit. ER nurses are dangerous. She opens a supply drawer and comes at me with a handful of IV fluids and syringes.

"Are you eating?"

"You mean food? Does cold pizza and beer count?"

"You should take care of yourself better."

"It's diarrhea. I'm full throttle."

"Poor thing. Just let me know if you want some of this." She puts the IV fluid in my face.

"Can I just drink it?"

"No, I'll need to start an IV."

Nurses would make good vampires.

After another trip to the bathroom, I'm back in the chart room hiding in the shadows. I just finished giving three reports to three different detox facilities, hoping someone will accept Robert and his wife. All they need is to be locked up for a few days and kept sober. There's no medical emergency. They would survive going home. Alcoholism is considered a disease. I disagree. It's an addiction to a substance caused by mental illness. A disease suggests helplessness. People can sober up on their own.

"You've got another one coming in." Shelly pokes her head around the corner and taps her fingernails on the door jamb.

"Think it will be a long night?"

"Three-day weekend, a full moon, disability checks just got mailed—you're going to be up all night!"

She says that with pleasure in her voice.

"And somehow you sound satisfied with that prediction, Shelly. Maybe you should work all night, too." I shoot her an evil smile.

"I'm off at midnight!"

The phones ring and she's gone. I can feel the electricity from the ER. I wasn't aware the moon was full this weekend. It's not just superstition that a full moon elevates human activity. Law enforcement, EMS, and fire departments frequently upstaff during full moons. Werewolves like to howl at full moons. I believe chaos resonates. That means when trouble starts, it multiplies quickly and spontaneously. Multiple-vehicle car accidents are a good example.

I wait as long as possible before reporting back to Dr. Mattia. He's hitting on all cylinders tonight. I'm feeling more removed from reality every minute. I'm quickly dehydrating, plus my OCD is ramping up. I'm starting to see shadows move and bugs crawling that aren't there. It's just my eyes playing tricks on me, but it means I'm tired. I'm tired as hell. I shouldn't be here tonight, but like I said, there's no good back-up plan. The other team members are long gone for the weekend, hiding at home with the phone turned off, and watching *COPS* reruns on TV.

"Stewart, I've got a patient I want you to see."

"Sure, Doc. I'm still waiting to hear about beds for Robert and his wife."

He hands a chart to a passing nurse. She replies, "Room Eight needs an IV, and Ten needs sutures."

"EMS in fifteen to twenty minutes with two patients! MVA on Highway 70, T-bone collision," someone reports to everyone and no one.

I'm back in the ER watching the chaos spin around me.

"At least it wasn't a head-on collision," I reply.

He doesn't laugh. He doesn't flinch. Dr. Mattia reminds me of Spock from *Star Trek*. If he does have emotions, no one here has ever seen them. But that's fine because an emotional reaction in an ER doesn't help much anyhow. Leave the sticky emotions to the patients. These are humans at their worst, bouncing off rock bottom after free-falling. Let them make an emotional mess, shit themselves, and puke on the floor. We'll give them a hot meal, some Ativan for anxiety, and send them home to do it all over again next weekend.

"If you could talk to the guy in Room Four, I think we could send him home."

And he's off to sew someone up and start an IV while waiting for two trauma patients to arrive. But I'm relieved because I was just told to pacify the patient with some cheap advice and tell him he can go home and continue his dysfunctional existence.

I knock on the door and step into a dark room with the chart in my hands. I haven't even looked at it yet because it appears the patient is not actively suicidal or homicidal. But I remind myself, lies run thick in an emergency room.

Someone is asleep in the bed. I turn on the light and look at the name on the chart. It's Marshall Winston again. A frequent flyer here, he's already finished a warm meal and turned in for the night.

"Marshall! It's Stewart. What the hell are you doing here? I thought you moved."

I sit down heavily and remove my glasses. I'm tired, yes, but I'm playing completely submissive as if the conversation won't be recorded and anything that is said will be off the record. He looks over his shoulder and rolls over to greet me.

"Dr. Stewart, I'm just having a hard time."

Marshall reminds me of Otis from *The Andy Griffith Show*. He has his own cell to use if he needs to sober up. I see Marshall more than any patient here.

"Why did you arrive in an ambulance, Marshall? That's unusual."

"My neighbors found me sleeping in my front yard. I guess they thought I was dead."

What a luxury to be able to drink until you pass out in your yard. Trained personnel arrive in fire trucks and ambulances. They rush you to a hospital and give you a nourishing meal, and all for free. Only in America do we encourage such parasitic behavior. I see a butter knife on his food tray and consider stabbing him multiple times.

"How much did you drink today, Marshall?" His BAC was .34 two hours ago. A quick 12-pack of beer would get you there. I suddenly think of Leroy. He's probably playing quarters with Cassandra by now with the same blood alcohol level. I look at my watch; it's 10:30 PM. The ER is a black hole now, pulling in chaos from the community, swallowing anything that isn't tied down. Sarah pokes her head in the door.

"You two doing alright?"

I laugh. She knows Marshall better than I do. What's funny is she just threw me into the bed with him. Who's the patient here? Maybe I look as bad as I feel. I glance at my reflection in my glasses.

"How about a banana bag?" She smiles, then disappears.

"For who?" She's looking forward to sticking me with a needle.

Marshall is still thinking about what day it is and how much he drank. "I drank two bottles of wine today."

"Well, Marshall, the good news is wine has some nutritional value. The bad news is we can't help you much tonight."

"I know, I know. I have to get control of my life and take responsibility for my actions."

I'm still looking at my reflection in my glasses. My nose looks really big. I wonder if men have nose plastic surgery.

"That's a good idea, Marshall. I think I read that in a textbook somewhere."

He looks at me for the first time. He's not sure if I just gave him a compliment or threw him an insult. He quickly chooses compliment and sighs at his own wisdom.

"I need to spend more time at the Senior Center to stay sober."

I stop examining my nose to consider his choice of therapeutic interventions. Senior citizens are the backbone of the pharmaceutical industry. Senior centers are a mecca for pain pills. I just nod in agreement. Then I hear the trauma doors slide open and suddenly the ER is filled with the sounds of firemen and portable equipment. I can hear diesel engines idling in the ambulance bay and the faint smell of smoke from their uniforms saturates the room. I turn off the lights in Marshall's room and slowly sit down. He talks for twenty minutes, and I ignore every word, as I watch the chaos unfold.

FIVE

I close the bathroom door and fall against it, catching my breath. No one is in the Fast Track hallway for now. It's just me and my diarrhea. I walk slowly to my room, knowing I don't have time to lie down. I look in and see the familiar array of LED lights glowing from the instruments on the walls and electric bed. Surely the room is infested with contagious microbes, but I still want to sleep for a while. I wipe my face with a handkerchief. The ER is waiting. I have four patients to interview, four people to send to mental hospitals, or four people to release to go home of their own free will. Dr. Machinski is impatiently waiting for me to give him four lucid recommendations.

I'm polishing my glasses with my handkerchief as I approach Dr. Machinski. He's studying x-rays and leaps out of his chair when he sees me coming. Dr. Mattia is finishing dictation over the phone and is in another world, wrapping up his shift and getting ready to go home.

I mentioned before that Dr. Lowder has the energy of a 5-year-old jacked up on candy and caffeine. Well, Dr. Machinski is fresh out of medical school and works twice as fast. Evidently, taking the Hippocratic Oath is a natural stimulant.

"What do you have?" he asks, ready to save the world.

"Doc, I just walked in here. I'll need a few minutes to figure out what's going on."

"Okay." He sounds disappointed.

He looks me up and down and quickly realizes I have my head up my ass. He shifts into a summary of my four patients which I don't listen to. I nod my head like a cheap tree ornament. I'm hoping the information, through osmosis, will somehow reappear during my interviews.

"C'mon, Doc, I feel like puking on your shiny leather shoes. Let me go to sleep for twelve hours. I'll get back with you tomorrow."

"Cocaine abuser in Room Twelve. Suicide attempt in Room Thirteen. There's a woman in Room Six who appears highly delusional, and a guy in Room Eight who wants to go to detox."

I manage a smile. I'm old enough to be his father. "Give me a few minutes, Doc, and I'll have it figured out."

❊ ❊ ❊

The lights are on and there's no chair for me to sit in. I lean against the wall and adjust my glasses. I'm writing notes on my clipboard, but the patient takes little notice. He's 23 and high as a kite on cocaine.

"You smoked seven hundred dollars' worth of cocaine in the last twenty-four hours. How much is that in grams?"

"It was my entire disability check. Now I don't have any money for food."

If I had a baseball bat, I'd beat him over the head, hoping to rearrange his brain.

"Last I heard, a gram was a hundred dollars, right?"

I need a number so I can formulate a recommendation. Quantity matters. How many beers did you drink? How many pills did you take? If he doesn't know, then the dealer might have ripped him off and sold him a 1-gram cocaine rock. Not that smoking a gram of cocaine is harmless, but it's less heinous than two or three grams in twenty-four hours.

"It was six grams. I watched him weigh it." He starts crying.

I did my undergraduate studies in Colorado during the '80s. I saw plenty of cocaine. If he had said three grams, I was going to call him a dumbass and try to send him home with some outpatient treatment suggestions.

"Wow," spills out of my mouth, as I slowly shake my head. I drop my clipboard to my side and examine him closely. He's thin but not malnourished.

"What's your disability?"

"I'm bipolar." He's wiping his face with both shirtsleeves. The tears keep coming.

"That's tough."

He looks at me, maybe sensing some compassion, maybe wanting to start an argument about how bipolar is real to him and not just frequent mood swings.

"It sucks." He sobs.

"Have you tried prescription medication?"

"It made me feel crazy."

"It takes time to get the dosage correct. People have told me it works if you are willing to work with a good psychiatrist."

"I see Dr. Hamrick."

"He's an idiot. He's a pediatrician acting like a psychiatrist. Try someone else." I step into the doorway and catch Sarah by the arm.

"Does this guy look hungry to you?"

"This isn't a restaurant!" She hurries away.

I turn and face him with the best quick advice I can think of. "You are self-medicating and doing a bad job. If you can find a medication that works, you won't need any cocaine. Plus, you will have money for food."

"I'll kill myself if you let me go. I have a gun, and I'll use it."

I look into his desperate eyes. People that suffer from true bipolar disorder love to be manic. Who wouldn't? Coming down from the mania is depressing and causes suicidal ideations. Superman one day, and the next, Eeyore the donkey looking for his lost tail.

"I'm not surprised. I'll make sure you get some help."

"Don't send me to Oakwood Hospital! Those people are crazy."

Everyone has a definition for crazy.

I go to the nurses' desk and wait for Sarah to cycle around. CJ looks up from her computer.

"Can you imagine smoking six grams of cocaine?" I'm still dumbfounded.

"He was probably trying to have a heart attack. He's lucky to be alive."

Sarah comes back and puts both hands on the counter for support. She's nearly out of breath.

"When was the last time you smoked six grams of cocaine?"

"Is that a lot?"

I stammer a little and shift my weight to the other foot. "Well, I once read that one gram is enough to satisfy four recreational-drug users."

"So, he smoked enough for a room full of twenty-four drug users."

"Something like that."

"Where do you get this information, Stewart?"

"*High Times* magazine. You should get a subscription."

"Why bother. I have you!"

More mindless bantering. It can go on for hours. But it's also an exchange of valuable information. After all, people that run AA meetings are no strangers to alcohol. The next time Sarah encounters a crackhead who tried to overdose, she will better understand who she is dealing with.

With the interview fresh on my mind, I go to Dr. Machinski and give him my recommendation. He has less need for me than any of the doctors that work in this ER, but he puts up with me because it's policy. It's policy to get a second opinion from a mental health professional so no one goes home and shoots themselves. He once disagreed with my decision to let someone go home and the patient stayed in the ER for about fifteen hours, waiting for a mental hospital to accept him. Nobody wanted to admit the guy. He didn't meet criteria. Finally, CJ intervened and told him we couldn't keep feeding him indefinitely. Go home and try a little harder to kill yourself. The system has no room for whiners.

I look at my watch; it's 1:15 AM. I think about Leroy for a moment. He and OB are probably spooning on my couch with all the doors open. I'm back in the chart room having an out-of-body experience. I have three patients to interview and little do I know, three more are on the way. I won't see my hospital bed until the sun rises. It's moments like these, I figure, when talking to someone who wants to die is comforting. No matter how bad I feel, they feel worse.

e patient's room and take immediate notice of all the ⏟ on her wrists. I walk up to her bedside and lean over, ⏟ting the stitches.

"Dr. Machinski does good work. I count twenty stitches. Is that right?" No accusations, no blame, just simple math that she can focus on.

She nods her head slowly, seemingly in shock, examining her own handiwork with her fingers. Her forehead is covered with superficial cuts that didn't need sewn together. She's 28 and appears healthy and well nourished. I notice she's attractive and probably takes good care of herself. If a homeless drunk living under a bridge did this it might make some sense, but she has a story to tell. A relentless thought or a perverted family member drove her to attack herself with a sharp object in hopes of ending the emotional pain.

"What did you use?"

She doesn't look up. "A pair of scissors."

Not my first choice of carving tools. I don't think I even own a pair of scissors. Why didn't you just use a sharp knife, I want to ask. Cutting your wrists could be life threatening if you can maintain a heavy flow of blood. Usually what happens is the laceration is clean and the vessels have an opportunity to spontaneously close. Lots of dramatic blood at first, then it stops. I look at her forehead again. She wanted her pain to be seen. She wanted to advertise the emotional trauma. She wanted someone to acknowledge the demon locked inside her head.

"Why did you cut your forehead?"

She moves her fingers to her head and carefully assesses the damage. She has a pretty face. The scars won't go away. She'll need some cosmetic surgery if she wants to hide the evidence of this night.

"Oh God!" she cries. "What have I done?"

"Think about it. Why did you cut your forehead? It's important."

She looks up at me. I'm still standing close to her bed. I want her to know that I'm not afraid of her, that her violent attack on her own flesh has nothing to do with me. Her lips quiver, she struggles with an answer. The pain is buried deep, so deep she had to turn to self-mutilation to be heard. Now she's in an emergency room, ready to be sent to a mental hospital to be further studied and sedated.

I look over my shoulder to see if anyone is watching. The ER is churning on its own, it's boiling now, boiling with trauma and chaos. I'm alone for a moment, alone with my patient. I'm wielding my axe, her skull is split, her brain is visible. I want the truth. I want to hear her thoughts and taste the horror crawling through her mind.

"Think about it!" I raise my voice to a loud whisper. "Why did you attack your face?"

Unorthodox, unethical, unkind? Maybe, but maybe not. She's vulnerable. Her psyche is exposed. I could make permanent suggestions. I could plant a heinous neurosis or a subtle psychosis. She might leave here strangely afraid of golf courses or suddenly bloom into a serial killer after six months of harmless clean living. Her eyes are filled with tears. Her bloody arms are trembling. She's emotionally fractured and capable of only sentence fragments. I lean even closer.

"My husband," she manages. The tears pour and her face is soaked.

I withdraw my attack and quietly sit down. I want to hide; I try to hide. I want her to forget I'm here so the wicked thoughts can flow freely, so some of the pain can pour on the floor for a custodian to mop up.

"No one in my family trusts me."

I'm not here to take away pain. I'm just here to give a recommendation. Are you mentally stable and can we send you home tonight, or do you need further treatment before you can face society again without wanting to kill yourself or others? In other words, are you a threat to people or property?

"No one supports my decisions."

She will survive. She won't do this again. Some medication, a few years of therapy.

"It's killing me to live with a husband that isn't supportive."

I'll find a country club rehab facility. Maybe I'll visit her frequently.

She looks me in the eye. Suddenly she looks possessed. Her voice changes. It gets deep and forceful. "If you let me go, I'll do it again!"

My daydream stops. I stand up and drop my clipboard. Maybe she will require more than a few years of therapy. Some mental illness lasts a lifetime, unfortunately. It's not just about someone having a bad day or a bad attitude. It's a daily struggle to get a grip on reality.

"I'll talk to Dr. Machinski. I'll see what I can do."

And I leave her to dwell in her private nightmare, picking at the fresh sutures on her wrists as I leave the room. I immediately go to Dr. Machinski so I can give him a lucid report. If I'm not careful I'll mix personal reactions with objective recommendations. It's about time to put on a strong coffee buzz to get me through the night. As dehydrated as I am, I should be high as a kite after the second cup. I find him exiting a patient room, removing sterile gloves. He's still wide awake and ready to take on the world.

"Hey, Doc!"

He gives me ten seconds of his time. I think fast.

"The lady in Room Thirteen is crazy as hell. I'll find her a bed somewhere."

He smiles and hurries away. Frequently the details don't matter here. Are you dead or dying? Are you suicidal or not? But in this case, I want to talk to the family to see if they have a diagnosis. She fooled me for a moment. How severe is her mental illness? Is her husband equally mentally ill? Maybe I could take out IVC papers on him, question him about abusive tendencies and childhood shortcomings. He's probably having an affair. She knows he's cheating. She just hasn't caught him yet.

I pass by Shelly at the reception desk. She knows I'm on a mission. I go through automatic double swinging doors into the waiting room. Beep, beep, announces the motion detector. Three security guards drinking coffee at their station casually look me over. I go to them; they are familiar with my tactics.

"Did any family come in with the lady who cut her wrists?"

"Sure did. They left shortly after they got here."

I lean on their counter, obviously frustrated. I look down at my clipboard and try to piece the puzzle together. They sense my frustration. The security guard talking to me is Hank. He's a retired state trooper.

"Who was with her? I mean, what family members were here?"

"Her husband, son, and daughter."

The family knew the drill. They knew she wouldn't be coming home. Evidently, her suicidal tendencies have been going on for a while. But to leave so quickly, without more information or further instructions? They don't even know where I'm going to send her. Like a sick animal at the veterinarian's office, they just told us to put her down and mail the bill. I consider both sides of the situation for a moment: she's tired of them, and they are tired of her. I turn to go to the chart room. It's time to make some phone calls to the psychiatric hospitals. I have two suicidal patients on my hands, and both of them told me they would try it again if given the chance.

"Maybe they will call tomorrow," I mumble as I walk away.

Back in the ER, I take a quick break at the nurses' station. It's merely a section of the big round counter in the middle of the room, but the nurses claim the 8-foot area as their own. The doctors share the same territorial mentality.

I'm leaning on the counter, pale and perspiring, when Sarah stops and looks at me.

"Can you go home?"

I manage a smile.

"I'm not even sure if I have health insurance, Sarah. My new employer hasn't paid me in weeks."

She's immediately concerned for a couple of reasons. One being that a good crisis counselor is hard to find. Without someone like me, the ER will back up like a toilet, clogged with mental patients.

Sarah shakes her head. "All the hospital has to do is take over the contract! Then you would work for us…and have health insurance!"

"That's too easy. Besides, this saves someone money. Maybe the CEO just bought a new Mercedes."

She thinks for a moment. I sip on my coffee and look over her shoulder into one of the trauma rooms. Blood and bandages—it doesn't look like one of mine.

"He drives a BMW. If you have diarrhea, coffee won't help."

"I feel great."

"You look like hell."

"What do you suggest?"

"Some IV fluids and a stool sample to start. I can talk to Dr. Machinski."

"No!" I reply quickly. "Who's the ER Doc tomorrow?"

"Dr. Lowder."

"Which one?"

"Probably both."

I consider the idea for a moment. I've had twenty BMs in the last twenty-four hours. People used to die from untreated diarrhea. I need to be drinking Gatorade or heavy amounts of alcohol to kill the bacterial invasion.

"I'll think about it, Sarah. I'm just not ready to share a stool sample with you. An STD maybe, but not a stool sample."

Her eyes get big, and I wait to be slapped in the face.

"You wish!"

Sarah is divorced, or separated, or something. It's harmless flirting as far as I'm concerned. Maybe she sees it differently. Nurses see the world differently. Nurses think everyone needs a liter of IV fluid and a few milligrams of Ativan. She leaves me to my confusion and disappears into the trauma room.

❁ ❁ ❁

"I'm Stewart. Dr. Machinski wanted me to talk to you."

Her name is Sadie, and she's 65 years old. She doesn't appear to weigh much more than that. I sit down to gather my thoughts, which are few at the moment. Maybe Sadie can help me feel better about myself. Sadie has a history of paranoid schizophrenia. It appears that she's actively delusional. The nurses told me she's crazy.

Sadie pays no attention to me, and I'm not even sure if she noticed I entered the room. Schizophrenics hear voices. It's possible she didn't hear mine mixed in with all the others. I blow my nose into my handkerchief to see if she notices. She's sitting on the hospital bed in a gown, hugging her knees and rocking back and forth. I wave my handkerchief through the air as if shaking out the bugs that came out of my nose.

"Damn allergies! Those little mushrooms grow everywhere."

Sarah speeds by the door and gives me a dirty look.

Still no response from Sadie.

"Hey, Sadie. Why are you here?"

She continues to stare at the wall and rock back and forth. Suddenly she stops rocking. She heard me this time.

"I have a large mass in my abdomen and a severe toothache."

I'm a little surprised at her choice of words. Either she had a medical background in an earlier life or she's very fixated on her body. Anyone can learn the language if they spend enough time in the ER.

I see CJ at the nurses' station.

"Excuse me for a moment, Sadie."

I exit the room in need of vital information. "Hey CJ. Is Sadie a frequent flyer? I've never seen her before."

CJ looks at her medical record on the computer screen.

"She was here four years ago for abdominal pain. That's her only visit."

"Did she tell you about her tumor and toothache?"

CJ smiles. "The abdominal exam was negative, and we gave her some ibuprofen for the toothache."

"The EMS report said she was combative at the nursing home."

"They found her in the hallways with a bloody towel between her legs, poor thing. She was screaming and wouldn't let anyone help her."

"Umm...where did the blood come from?"

"It was vaginal."

"Is that normal? I mean, at her age?"

"It can be."

Sadie is rocking again when I return. I go to the chair and sit down heavily. Now I can have a conversation. I have cues to prompt her with. The schizophrenia consciousness is full of noise. You have to ask the right questions to get through the interference.

"What's going on at the nursing home, Sadie?"

This time she doesn't stop rocking. "They neglect me. The staff is abusive."

"The paramedics found you screaming with a bloody towel between your legs. Where did the blood come from, Sadie?"

She doesn't answer at first. Then she repeats the complaint about the abdominal mass and the toothache.

"Thanks, Sadie."

I go back to the nurses' station to sort out the details. Silently I stare at my clipboard and occasionally look up to watch the chaos. I am deaf and mute for the moment. The staff has learned to ignore my quirks. CJ is entering data into the computer. Sarah stops to catch her breath.

"Call me crazy, but it's my job to ask crazy questions."

"I wouldn't want your job," Sarah replies.

"I don't know how you do it," CJ adds.

"Is it possible Sadie was raped?" I ask.

They silently toy with my theory, juggling the uncomfortable thought. CJ types silently and Sarah looks past me with faraway eyes. ER nurses leave no stones unturned.

"Even if that's true, it would be impossible to prove. She's not a valid historian," Sarah summarizes.

"And maybe it was consensual," CJ responds.

"Who would we report that to?" I cringe.

"She does have a urinary tract infection. That could cause some bleeding." Then Sarah adds, "Looks like you have some more phone calls to make!"

"Let me know what you decide." CJ smiles.

Schizophrenia mixed with old age, it's a bad recipe for human rights. Sadie was eventually admitted upstairs for further medical observation. Her UTI kept her out of a mental hospital and kept me off the phones trying to place her in one.

As for my theory, it was just another cheap theory. Emergency rooms don't have the resources to run rape tests. If this was a television show, lots of people would have cared, and lab results would have been found in fifteen minutes. My job is to rid the ER of the mentally ill, to empty examination rooms and gurneys, and to make room for trauma patients and medical emergencies. Emergency rooms weren't designed for a daily tsunami of mental illness.

SIX

I hear a knock on the door. I've fallen asleep sitting on the toilet. My pants are still around my ankles, and I have no idea what time it is. I focus on my watch: it's 3:30 in the morning. This time tomorrow morning I'll be well on my way to finishing my three-day shift. I'll be sound asleep in my hospital bed, while the ER will be churning with medical emergencies and trauma patients who don't matter to me in the least. Are you suicidal or not? That's all that matters to me. Go home and try again.

"How much did you drink today? I mean, starting yesterday when you woke up?"

"I drank a bottle of whiskey and an eighteen-pack of beer."

Some people would respond with "I don't know," or "I don't remember."

"Wow! You have some serious tolerance to alcohol." His blood alcohol level is .255 and he's moderately impaired but not drunk. His name is Robert and he is 37 years old. Dr. Machinski ordered IV fluids. Robert is on his third liter of normal saline. Normal saline is a neutral sterile solution of water and electrolytes. Alcohol dehydrates the body. IV fluids quickly rehydrate the blood and tissues.

Robert isn't a binge drinker. A binge drinker doesn't count drinks. They don't monitor their alcohol intake. Robert drinks with determination. He counts every shot and every beer and keeps track of how many beers are left in the refrigerator or how many shots are in the bottle. He stays at home while drinking, maybe by himself, maybe with an occasional visitor. Alcoholics at this level won't offer you a drink if you stop by. Bring your own! That's why Leroy drinks Milwaukee's Best—because no one else will.

"When was the last time you were sober for any length of time?"

"I've been drinking this way for over a year. I went to detox about a year ago, and that was the last time I was sober."

Drug and alcohol detox facilities are surprisingly ineffective. It takes more than a few days or weeks to get alcohol to release its grip. Alcohol rewires the brain, creating a need or desire. Like a parasite, alcohol will take over your body and force you to keep it alive.

I decide to go for the jugular vein. There's no need to waste time at this hour. I still have three more patients to see.

"It's going to be hard to find you a bed anywhere."

"I know."

"You would be amazed at how many people need the same help."

"I was here two weeks ago. They couldn't find a bed then either."

Robert apparently hasn't responded well to detox treatment. A detox facility sobers you up by locking you up, but most people start drinking again. If you show up a second and third time, they will simply put you at the back of the line. And the lines are long.

I stand up to go. Robert appears genuinely remorseful. I have a desire to lecture him about how drinking like a fish is a luxury that most people can't afford. I want to pull the needle out of his arm and save the IV fluid for someone who is really dying. I want to slap him a few times and tell him to get his shit together because thousands of idiots just like him all across the country are clogging up emergency rooms.

"I'll see if I can find you a bed somewhere. But if I can't, are you able to go home?"

Robert starts to answer, but I interrupt him. "In other words, are you going to hurt yourself if we let you go home?"

I normally wouldn't be so unprofessional, but he's a professional drinker and another day won't matter. It won't even matter if he goes home and drinks for two more weeks. We're open 24/7. Asking someone if they are going to hurt themselves simply puts the thought in their head so they can make a decision. Robert may have no desire to die. He's just addicted to alcohol. Now he's thinking about whether death is a good solution.

"No. I'll be okay."

Robert knows how our system works. He's already resigned himself to another day of pulling on the bottle and smashing empty cans on his forehead. Maybe he came to the ER to get IV fluid therapy and a warm meal. Maybe he has insurance, maybe not; it doesn't matter. Either way, the American taxpayer will pay the bill. We will help and enable these patients until the Statue of Liberty falls into the ocean. Only then will we look away and say, "Help yourself. We can't afford to help any longer. Our system is bankrupt."

"I'll see what I can do, Robert."

I'm as frustrated as he is. He wants help. I can't give him any. This is Labor Day weekend, and it would be easier to schedule a 9:00 AM tee time than to find a psychiatrist who's willing to sign over care for another drunk.

"Look, if I can't find a bed at a detox facility, don't give up. Come back tomorrow. We'll be here."

❀ ❀ ❀

The ER is its own world. It's happening on another planet. Everyone looks alien to me, and the commotion is constant now. It makes me think of a playground at an elementary school, but the difference is everyone is dying, not playing, and the toys are portable x-ray machines and IV pumps, not harmless rubber balls. I hear a patient moaning in pain, another yelling about something, and still a third one lets out a scream. The staff is running full throttle. Every bed is filled.

I just got off the phone giving detailed reports and faxing lab results to nearby psychiatric hospitals. I have to get my patients out of the ER in a hurry. Vacant beds mean lives can be saved. A trauma patient can't wait for a suicidal patient to get it together. Mental illness is a luxury at this hour.

Dr. Machinski is in a trauma room helping with a cardiac arrest. CJ hangs up the EMS phone and looks up at me. I'm leaning on the counter and trying to stay out of the way. I have my clipboard and pen in my hands. A nurse walks by. Her name is Linda. I lash out and hit her over the head with the edge of the clipboard. The pain is so intense her legs buckle and she falls to her knees. I wield my pen and stab her in the neck, tearing her jugular vein. Four people scream at once and rush toward me.

"What's up?" CJ is staring at me.

I watch Linda walk away and disappear into the trauma room.

"Do you think there are any mind-readers in here?"

"Why? Do you need one?"

Low blood sugar, lack of sleep, maybe I need some caffeine. I need to go home and wake up Leroy and start drinking. Of course, there won't be any left. The trash can will be full of empty beer cans surrounded by plastic grocery bags full of smelly tuna cans. If I want to have beer for breakfast, I'll have to find a gas station willing to break the Sunday morning no-beer-sales law. I already know where to go. A former patient works the register. He was suicidal a few months ago.

CJ hands me IVC papers and nods toward Room 13. "Dr. Machinski mentioned detox, but there's no way he's leaving the hospital."

I look over my shoulder at my next patient. He's passed out on his side with an IV of normal saline running fast. I look for the blood exam report.

"Holy shit!" I whisper aloud. "His BAC is .424!"

"And it was probably higher before he got here."

CJ is one of the most level-headed people I've ever met. Aside from smoking a pack of cigarettes a day, she seems very stable. Never too high or too low, she would be the last person to end up here as a patient.

I look at him again. "Is he alive?"

"Hardly. The family got worried and went to the magistrate. He's been binging for three weeks, according to them, and not eating or sleeping."

"Where's the deputy?" I look around the ER.

"There's an MVA out on the highway. He went to help."

In other words, the drunk in Room 13 isn't your patient yet, and the drunk who just caused an accident on the highway isn't your patient either. He will be a medical emergency until further notice. A flood of relief spills over me. It's almost 5:00 AM, and I only have two patients to go. Five AM is the magic hour. It's the time of morning when mental illness goes to sleep. It's statistically the time when the drugs and alcohol have run out and the body, no matter how intoxicated, is asking for sleep or a warm meal. I rarely get new patients between 5:00 AM and noon. If someone goes to the ER at those hours with acute mental illness, it's usually because a prescription ran out and they don't want to lose another night of sleep. Acute mental illness takes its time. It doesn't take as long to turn homicidal.

"Wake up. My name is Stewart. Dr. Machinski wants me to talk to you."

I raise the head of his bed so he is forced to listen to me. He opens his eyes but doesn't move.

"What is your name?"

"James."

"Do you know where you are?"

He thinks for a moment. "Emergency room."

"James, could you tell me what day it is?"

"Sunday morning." He moves his head, trying to look at me, then gives up.

I notice his face and hands are swollen. James is 36 so it's probably not due to heart failure. James has successfully turned off his liver and kidneys with alcohol abuse, and maybe a few more organs as well. The silly questions I just asked him are a test to determine his orientation. Delivered in different ways, the exam looks for cognitive functioning and whether the patient has a grip on reality. As a paramedic, a response to pain was sometimes all you would get from the exam. James knows who he is, where he is, the day of the week, and the time of day. All that put together means I can have a brief conversation with him until he passes out again.

"Your family is worried about you, James."

"I don't feel human," he responds.

"Why have you been drinking so much, James? Are you trying to kill yourself?"

A long minute goes by, and I decide he has fallen asleep. Then he answers the question. "No, but I wish I was dead based on how bad I feel."

Binge drinking is interesting. It's not the same as Robert's methodical approach to drinking a bottle of whiskey a day or Leroy's dedication to Milwaukee's Best beer. Binge drinkers are typically sober and only binge occasionally. They don't drink anything for days and weeks, then suddenly lose complete control and nearly drink themselves to death. Binging only happens with alcohol. If you binge on pills, it's called an overdose. If you binge on cocaine, it's called expensive. If you binge on marijuana, it's called getting baked, toasted, or fried off your ass. No one has ever died of a marijuana overdose.

An alcohol binge can kill you. Alcohol has medicinal value at low levels. Ancient civilizations unearthed by archaeologists always reveal evidence of fermentation vessels. Jesus turned water to wine, not wine to water, but alcohol ingestion at high levels quickly turns to poison. The human body can only process one drink per hour according to studies.

I leave the room without saying anything else. James will be sent upstairs to the ICU for a few days so his organs can start working again. I might get called in to talk to him again. It will be my job once again to determine if he can go home safely or go to a psychiatric unit at another hospital. James will binge again, either way. This short visit won't cure him. He is dancing with the devil for sure, but it will take incarceration from a deadly MVA or an alcohol coma to quit abusing alcohol.

"Two more patients, right? Who's next?" I'm back at the nurses' station with Sarah and Linda. CJ is outside smoking a cigarette. I'm developing a false sense of hope, thinking that I might get some sleep soon.

"Do you want to talk to a cocaine abuser or a guy who tried to shoot himself?" Sarah asks, not looking up and holding the counter for support. She looks pissed off about something.

"How can you only try to shoot yourself?" I ask.

"The gun didn't go off," Linda responds.

"That's embarrassing. How about I send the cokehead to detox and the gunslinger home so he can try again?"

Sarah looks up but doesn't smile.

"What's your problem? You look like you need a few milligrams of Ativan, Sarah."

"Dr. Machinski is so damn slow. He can't make a decision about anything!"

I look around the ER. Every bed is full. The entire staff appears confused. I see a nurse dancing with an IV pole and another trying to defibrillate himself. Dr. Machinski is crying like a baby, trying to push a syringe with an 18-gauge needle through his eye. A security guard rushes at him and they both go tumbling into a supply cart. The sound of metal trays and plastic bottles bouncing on the white linoleum floor is deafening.

"It looks like a family reunion in here!" Sarah marches away with IV tubing in one hand and a liter of normal saline in the other.

I blink and see Dr. Machinski reading a chart, flipping through pages of lab results and notes. He's being careful not to make any hasty decisions. Linda winks at me and walks away. I hurry into Room 13 to interview another drug addict.

"So, you're here voluntarily? That's a little unusual at this hour."

I'm sitting next to Gary, watching bugs crawl across the walls. If I look directly at them, they go away. It's my peripheral vision creating the visual hallucination. I'm trying to remain calm and hope it doesn't get much worse. Gary is high on cocaine and wants help so he can quit snorting cocaine.

"Have you ever smoked cocaine? Crack cocaine, right? You melt down the powdered cocaine into a rock then smoke it, right?"

"No. I just snort it."

"But snorting cocaine isn't very efficient. I mean, some of it goes down your esophagus into your stomach. I'm surprised you haven't graduated into smoking cocaine."

Gary wasn't expecting a conversation like this. He assumed the ER staff wouldn't have any idea what he was involved with. He assumed he would seamlessly move from an ER bed to a detox bed and get three hot meals and a bed for a week—three hots and a cot, we call it. I look at my watch; it's 5:30 AM. Gary is 24 and he spent the night abusing cocaine. He wasted his federal government disability check on illegal drugs and now he wants food and shelter, courtesy of the local taxpayers.

"Your chart says you have a history of depression and Tourette's syndrome. Is that how you get disability?"

Gary grows impatient with my line of questioning. He's still fully dressed and squirms in the hospital bed. It's a little unusual he doesn't have a gown on and a prophylactic IV started in case a medical emergency presents itself. Cocaine abuse and cardiac arrest frequently go together. It's a clear statement from the nurses that he is hiding something, masking the truth and presenting a fictitious alibi, wasting our time and taking up valuable space.

"I just want to be locked up so I can quit snorting cocaine!"

I swat at a fly buzzing past my face. It may have been real, I'm not sure.

"I want to die. I just want to kill myself!"

Gary just raised his voice. It means he wants to take control of the conversation. It means he is afraid of the direction the conversation is going. Anger is the invention of fear. Gary expressed anger because he is fearful. He is fearful because he is high on drugs and isn't getting what he wants.

"What do you want from us, Gary? I don't even understand how you can afford to abuse cocaine. It's not like you have a job that pays for your habit."

Gary is confused for a long moment trying to digest my callous response. As tired as I am, I'm not going to let a counterfeiter tax an ER staff that is already running on fumes. I'm calling his bluff.

Gary contorts in the bed and raises both hands in frustration. He shakes his head, trying to say something meaningful, but no words escape his mouth.

"Fine! Then let me go. I just want to get out of here," he manages.

But not home. He has no plan to go home because he is currently homeless. He throws back the blanket, and I stand up. CJ is at the door and John, another nurse, is quickly at her side.

"It looks like Gary wants to discharge himself," I casually announce.

CJ takes charge in her kind but forceful way.

"Gary, relax. We will let you go, but Dr. Machinski has to sign a release order. Are you hungry?"

Does Gary need help? Yes, he does. Does Gary need help from the local ER at 5:30 in the morning? No, he doesn't.

Gary has chronic issues, and he made a desperate decision, wanting to escape his demons of poverty and impulsivity. He was hoping to hide in our robust mental health system and get a clean bed and some free food.

"Excuse me. I have a gunslinger to talk to."

Just because you announce publicly that you want to die doesn't guarantee help. There are over 7 billion humans consuming air, water, and food, and contrary to some religious beliefs, 99.99% of the population doesn't make any contribution. If you want to die, then you can talk about it, or attempt it, your free choice. One is called suicidal ideations and the other attempted suicide. Thousands of people have suicidal ideations that go away. Your local emergency room may or may not have time to help you entertain your fantasy.

I make some quick phone calls, then hurry back to the ER to interview Michael the gunslinger. I'm experiencing a brief adrenaline rush, as I'm feeling comfortable that he will be my last patient for a few hours. I'm excited because I can pass out in my hospital bed soon. I can get a few hours of sleep before starting the second half of my three-day shift.

I look at my watch: it's 6:00 on Sunday morning. I'm sitting in Michael's room and he's asleep. The lights are off and the door is open, so plenty of light is pouring across the floor. I lean forward and watch the ER for a few minutes. The chaos is subsiding. Dr.

Machinski made decisions and patients were transferred to ICU, SICU, surgery, med floor, radiology, or released. The nurses are still moving fast but not running, and the noise level has dropped significantly. Michael danced with the devil for sure, and I'm ready to hear his sordid tale.

I shuffle the paperwork on my clipboard and clear my throat. He is lying on his back with the bed slightly inclined. He opens his eyes.

"Hey, Michael. It's me, Stewart."

I recognize Michael from a prior visit to the ER. The last time I interviewed him, he was suffering acute depression and drinking heavily. He and his girlfriend were walking beside the highway when she was struck by a car and killed. It would be a hell of a thing to have to watch. He sits up quickly and throws his legs over the side of the bed, leaning on his hands. Michael is ready to talk about his near-death experience.

"Tell me what happened."

Michael shakes his head, then laughs softly. "It didn't go off. It was my gun, and it didn't go off." He looks me in the eye. "Dr. Stewart, I've fired that gun a hundred times, and it has never misfired."

It's a good time for me to say nothing. I nod my head. He continues in a loud whisper.

"So I ejected the bullet and put another one in the chamber. And the same thing happened! Twice in a row!"

"What kind of gun are we talking about?"

"A nine-millimeter automatic. I put it under my chin like this." He shapes his hand into a gun and puts the barrel under his jaw, pointing upward toward his cervical spine and brain.

It hardly matters why Michael wanted to kill himself. He obviously tried...twice. He is suffering acute depression from a traumatic loss. I remember clearly from the first interview that he said he loved her. What is interesting to me is why the gun didn't go off, and I'm not alone because he is fixated on the same answer.

"It didn't go off twice!" he repeats himself. "I shouldn't be here, Dr. Stewart."

I'm in awe. The guts, the willpower, the nerve, the courage, the stupidity it would require to try such a thing—twice! I want to ask him how old the ammunition was or the methods he uses to clean and oil his gun, but those details don't matter either.

"Why didn't you try again?"

"My girlfriend found me and took away the gun."

"Your girlfriend was hit by a car."

"I have a new girlfriend."

I adjust my glasses and take a deep breath. Serial monogamy is popular. Michael apparently doesn't like to be alone.

Suddenly I hear a food tray fall to the floor and someone yelling. It's Gary. He's tired of waiting for Dr. Machinski to discharge him. I lean forward and see him marching out of the ER waving his arms.

"Fuck this place!" And he goes through the sliding doors into the ambulance receiving dock. It's not a good choice of exits because any number of EMS and law enforcement personnel can be out there smoking cigarettes and relaxing between calls. Three nurses follow him out the door. Soon I hear more yelling, then it grows quiet. Michael is watching the scene with the same interest. It's at that point I remember he has a 3-year-old daughter with a former girlfriend.

Within minutes the nurses return through the sliding doors with CJ leading. All three are grinning ear to ear.

"The police just arrested him for vandalizing the ambulance dock!" CJ says to Sarah. Everyone throws their hands in the air in celebration, then it's over. They go back to work like nothing happened. Gary got his wish: three hots and a cot, plus a misdemeanor. He was determined not to go back to the streets tonight.

"Listen to me, Michael." I stand up and get his full attention, and he surprises me by standing up too. He is 31 and tall, so I have to look up a little. "You are still alive because your daughter needs you."

My words sink in and he lowers his eyes, thinking.

I go to Dr. Machinski and give him my recommendations, then to the nurses' station with my updates. Ten minutes later I'm in my sacred hospital bed, fully clothed with my shoes still on and clipboard in my hand, passed out cold.

SEVEN

Someone opens the door then shuts it. I listen to the intruder walk away. Focusing on the background noise, I hear a phone ring and the movement of people across the sterile floors, but the ER sounds relatively quiet. I raise my hand and hold my watch in front of my face. The room is glowing red and green from the LED lights on the medical equipment. I'm not intubated, and no one mistakenly started an IV on me, but I feel as good as dead. It's 9:15 in the morning. I slept less than three hours.

A wave of panic rushes over me. I'm still on call until tomorrow, Monday at 5:00 PM. I sit up and swing my legs over the side. I desperately need a shower and some food. I'm dirty, I smell bad, and my teeth feel fuzzy. I'm not a praying man, but I ask out loud for peace and quiet until the sun sets.

"Give me hell when the sun goes down, but let me rest until then, please."

My first goal is to check the status of the ER. Do I have any patients waiting or soon to arrive? Is EMS working a call? Is it a drug overdose or attempted suicide? Maybe the sheriff just broke up a domestic fight and someone is acutely depressed. Hangovers can trigger psychotic meltdowns. Too many bowel movements can cause hallucinations.

I grab my mouthwash and tiptoe across the hallway to the bathroom. Moments later I rush through the ER like I'm late for a plane and I need to get to the airport. The staff changed at 7:00 AM, and I don't know the day nurses very well. I smile at everyone, tap my clipboard with my pen as if thinking clearly, then nearly run out the doors and across the parking lot to my yellow Jeep. Before long I'm driving south along the sandy coast to my condo on the overgrown golf course. This is the absolute worst part of a shift, driving home while still on call. More than anything you want to make it home, but the possibility of having to make a U-turn and return to the ER is very good. And the closer you get to the front door the worse the anxiety gets. By the time I turn into my parking lot, I'm hyperventilating and sweating profusely.

Then I remember Leroy.

I park the Jeep and take a deep breath. The phone hadn't rung yet. I just might have time to get a shower and relax. I look up and see my front door is wide open, and OB is sitting on my porch looking at me. As I said before, Eddie doesn't allow pets unless you give him a hefty deposit. Scar cost me an arm and a leg. Rick is the only other person on the course who admits to having a pet, and his dog Molly showed up before the expensive pet rule. Eddie and Rick are friends of sorts anyhow. Rick manages a fancy restaurant and told me numerous stories about Eddie drinking too much and starting fights. Eddie keeps Rick close so he won't talk.

I get out of the Jeep and OB comes over to greet me. He puts his nose in my crotch, nearly knocking me down. I drop my briefcase and swear at him.

"Damnit, OB! You're not supposed to be outside!"

I hurry into the condo with OB at my heels. The back screen door is open too, and the entire downstairs smells like dirty socks and dog food. OB has one of my mixing bowls full of food, and a 50-pound bag of dog food on the floor next to it. I stand in awe. Leroy has my ironing board out and strewn across the top are three pairs of socks and some underwear. I'm doubtful that they were washed. My furniture is hidden by more clothing, and my highly organized desk has golf equipment spread out everywhere. I find a spot on the counter for my briefcase and open the refrigerator.

"Payday!" I laugh aloud. There's a fresh 18-pack of Milwaukee's Best and a mystery bag from McDonald's. Grease stains have soaked through the crumpled paper sack.

"Hey OB, have you seen Scar?"

I open a can and inhale it. Seconds later I'm having another. An average male my weight can have 2.5 drinks in one hour and still be legally sober. I'm going to make the most of it.

I go to the back porch just in time to meet Leroy as he speeds up in a golf cart. He slams on the brakes and pounds the steering wheel.

"You goddamn hound! Where have you been?"

"Are you talking to me?"

"I've been all over the golf course looking for you."

OB sits down and scratches at some kind of infestation.

"Hey Leroy, check this out."

I guzzle my second beer and belch. Leroy gets off the golf cart to further reprimand OB.

"Where did you get the golf cart?" I notice there aren't any clubs on it.

"I borrowed it from Eddie."

It's good to have friends as relaxed as Leroy. With the world so uptight about rules and regulations, Leroy has an amazing ability to ignore most of them.

"You told him you were looking for OB?"

"I told him I was staying with you, and my dog ran away."

Some things are better left unsaid.

"How long can you keep it? Maybe we should go play eighteen holes."

"Get your clubs. I'm ready."

I step inside and lean out the door. "I need a shower first."

"Are you still on call?"

I hold up my cell phone. "I'm hoping it will be quiet until this afternoon. I rarely get calls on Sunday mornings."

Leroy scratches OB behind the ears while OB kicks at the air. I go to get another beer.

"Did you see any crazy people last night?" Leroy inquires as I'm reaching into the refrigerator.

"Leroy, our lives are pretty normal compared to some people." I step outside and look up at the sun. The warmth feels good. I get to enjoy a moment of peace. Sometimes moments are all that's allowed.

"I had a patient last night that tried to shoot himself."

"How do you try to shoot yourself?" Leroy is a good listener when he wants to be.

"The gun misfired, not once, but twice."

I open my eyes and watch Leroy's reaction. He's as dumbfounded as anyone should be, imagining such insanity.

"Why didn't he try a third time?"

Which takes me back to Michael.

There is little research on treating suicidal ideations or what to say to someone after they tried to kill themselves. Most of the research, time, and energy goes into suicide prevention. The only studies I ever read concerning post-suicide attempts concluded the same simple ideas. It's a two-step process. Identify a talent or skill, then convince the patient they can use that talent or skill tomorrow if they decide to wake up alive.

Michael definitely got a quick transfer to a psychiatric hospital. Placement was easy. A sheriff's deputy transported him personally, handcuffed in the backseat of a patrol car. But why all the attention? Michael is no different from the thousands of other suicidal patients who saturate our emergency rooms across the country. He is unemployed and makes no measurable contribution to society. He collects food stamps and abuses alcohol when he can afford it.

The answer is disturbing—we have nothing better to do.

Try a thought experiment to prove this theory to yourself. Imagine you worked in an ER, but not in the United States. Imagine you worked in an ER in Baghdad, Iraq. Imagine the ER is bustling day and night with very serious level one trauma. If a patient showed up who tried to shoot themselves twice unsuccessfully, what would they do? They wouldn't have the resources to treat the patient. The available resources would be limited to saving the patients who were dying. Mental illness would take a backseat to life-threatening trauma, and the patient who tried to kill himself would sit in the hallway all night long and be asked to leave in the morning, to make room for more trauma patients.

Like substance abuse, mental illness is a luxury, and our country is overrun with both, but we still try as hard as we can to treat it.

Our mental health system is hemorrhaging, but it's not dead; it has a weak pulse and agonal breathing. If America is ever attacked by a foreign military or terrorists, then trying to shoot yourself won't matter much.

After taking a long shower, I weigh my options to see which makes more sense. I could go to bed and get some much-needed rest, or I could go play golf with Leroy. Maintaining my own mental health is paramount. I have a little more than twenty-four hours to go until I can turn the phone over to Felicity. She will work nights the rest of the week. Day coverage is done by various 8-to-5 counselors who have no idea how bizarre the ER gets after the sun sets. I'm exhausted, I'm dehydrated, but the shower woke me up and the beer feels good, so I grab my clubs.

"We can give the cart back to Eddie when we are done."

Leroy laughs because he had already made the same decision. He's just surprised I would think of it.

"He won't mind?"

"I play for free here, Leroy."

"But I bet that doesn't include a cart."

We strap our clubs down and head for the nearest tee.

"You know how much Eddie charged me for a pet deposit?" I tee up first and hit a line drive into the lake. The ball skips across the surface and buries into the muddy bank on the other side.

"I'll play that," I respond happily.

Leroy lines up three balls and hits all of them straight down the fairway. He looks satisfied.

"Three balls, three holes, that's nine holes of golf. My game has improved these last few days."

Leroy normally drinks a beer per hole, but I'm not sure how he will account for playing three balls at the same time. It's almost noon when we finish the third hole, number eighteen, right in front of the clubhouse. Eddie is on the porch, rocking in a chair. We drive up in the cart and park in front of him. I'm going to let Leroy start the conversation since he's driving.

"Did you find your dog?"

Leroy takes a drink of beer and wipes his mouth with his forearm. Empty cans litter the back of the cart. Beer has to be purchased in the clubhouse. You can't bring your own. Eddie makes a lot of money selling beer to shitty golfers.

"Yeah. Stupid hound. He was in the parking lot the whole time. Stewart found him before I did."

I nod at Eddie and sip on my beer. "How much do we owe you for the cart, Eddie?"

Eddie looks in both directions, wondering. "How many holes did you play?"

"I'm not sure," I reply. "I played three and Leroy played nine."

"Pay me for eighteen, and we'll be even."

Some deals are better than others.

On the way back to the condo my phone rings. It's the ER. My delusion of happiness and joy quickly disappears, and I sober up.

"This is Stewart."

"Emergency Room here. Dr. Lowder would like to speak with you," the ER receptionist announces with the emotion of a robot.

I look at Leroy. We are still in the golf cart. He has the Senior Tour on his mind. Another hundred holes of free golf and he'll be ready.

"Which Dr. Lowder?" I force a laugh.

"Michael Lowder."

"Sure. Put him on."

My phone is rerouted, and suddenly I'm in a holding pattern circling Dr. Lowder's airport. I look down and see numerous airplanes tangled together on the runway, burning, smoke billowing, flames reaching into the sky. Ten minutes later my arm is numb holding the phone against my head. Leroy is on his way back to the clubhouse with the cart, and I'm trying to change clothes using one hand.

Another five minutes pass, and he finally picks up the phone. To Dr. Lowder, the last fifteen minutes felt like one, as he just juggled six patients at once. I'm dressed and ready to go, standing in the kitchen and looking into my empty refrigerator.

"Dr. Lowder here."

"Hey, Doc, it's Stewart."

"Yes. Oh yes, I have a patient for you!" He sounds relieved, knowing he has help diagnosing the mentally ill patient. Like I said, doctors hate psychiatric medicine. I even heard a doctor once say that it was easy to identify the future psychiatrists in medical school. Evidently, they stand out.

"The name is Timothy Beacham, eighteen-year-old male."

"Oh God!" I interrupt. "I've seen him already this weekend."

"I'm not surprised. I don't think you need to come in. I just wanted to get your input on this kid."

A wave of relief rushes over me. I reach for another beer. Tonight will likely be hell unleashed at the ER, but I still have hope to get some more sleep. Once I make the 30-minute drive along the coastline to the hospital, I don't dare return home until the sun rises. Like vampires, the mentally ill come out at night.

"What's his chief complaint, Doc?"

"Suicidal ideations. He says he wants to die."

"That's what he usually says."

"I'll just give him some Ativan and send him home then."

"Call me if you need me, Doc."

I hang up, and the phone rings again. It's Cassandra.

"What's up, Cass?"

All I hear is loud music. Cassandra is trying to talk over her underground British punk band music. I hear her say the words bloody, cheeky, and Yankee, so I know she's having a good day. All I can do is throw in a few expressions like "no way" and "get real." She goes on for a few minutes, then pauses. The music is so loud I have to hold the phone away from my head.

"The ER has been crazy," I yell. "I'm on call until tomorrow at five PM. Be sure to come over. We can play strip poker with Leroy!"

"Sounds like a plan!" she yells back, then hangs up.

Some people you can't change. I don't even dare ride with her because her music is so aggravating. I climb the stairs to my bedroom. Sure enough, my cat Scar, who isn't allowed upstairs, is sound asleep on my bed with his head on my pillow. My skin crawls at the thought of all the cat hair that will end up on my clothing. I push the thought aside and fall fast asleep.

EIGHT

A bell rings. A church bell, a car alarm, maybe my smoke alarm. I open my eyes. I'm in my bed, spooning with Scar, and my cell phone is ringing. It's 5:15 PM. It seems the gates of hell have been opened.

"This is Stewart."

"This is the Emergency Room. Dr. Lowder would like for you to come in, to evaluate a patient."

"Which one?"

"Dr. Kevin Lowder."

"I'll be there in thirty minutes."

The three-day holiday weekend is just getting started for some. Tomorrow is Labor Day, and I'm not even sure what the holiday is supposed to be about. For people with mental illness, a change in routine can be very stressful. It gives a person more time to be depressed and suicidal.

The drive along the coast is peaceful. The sun is setting and the sky is a kaleidoscope of color. I'm far from rested. Just the opposite, I'm exhausted from forty-eight hours of crisis intervention. The ER staff continually rotates fresh workers in and out the doors, but our small team of two or three crisis counselors sees rest only when business is slow. Customers are endless. Everyone is a customer; some wait longer than others to have a meltdown. This time tomorrow I should be driving the other direction with a cold drink in my hand.

I notice right away the ER has a strange vibration, as I punch in the door code and enter the sterile linoleum and fluorescent catacomb. Mostly medical patients with fevers and chest pain, the trauma rooms are empty, and for the moment, I have just one mental health emergency to deal with.

Her name is Mary, and she is 52 years old. I'm sitting in her room, flipping through her chart, saying nothing. The sheriff's deputy is leaning on the counter at the nurses' station flirting. Mary is being held against her will by an involuntary commitment order signed by a local after-hours judge or magistrate: the IVC. If you are mad at your spouse and want to get even, try IVC papers. Make up a huge lie and be convincing. It will work every time.

Mary is apparently delusional. More than one nurse told me she was crazy as hell, which translated into a diagnosis means she is presenting with some very obvious and bizarre behavior.

I adjust my glasses numerous times and make odd sounds, like I have something lodged in my throat. I launch into a fit of scratching and slap my arm as if attacking a herd of bugs.

"What's going on, Mary?"

She's having trouble ignoring me and is watching my odd conduct out of the corner of her eye. Mary looks well nourished but somewhat unkempt. Her clothes don't match or fit well, and her hair is a mess. I slap my arm again. I want to be on her team.

"Terrorists," she whispers.

I stand up quickly and wipe off the chair with my hand, then sit down and adjust my glasses again.

"They are everywhere, you know?" I reply, whispering.

"I made an alarm system they can't get through."

"Wow! That's great, Mary. What kind of alarm system?"

"I have fishing line running all through the house, so if anyone enters, I'll hear something move."

"Very cool, Mary. I hadn't thought of that." I take out my handkerchief and remove my glasses. Slowly and methodically, I begin dusting my face. "What test line do you use?"

"Thinner the better."

"I have some eight-pound test at home."

"That would work," she assures me.

I clear my throat a few times and carefully fold my handkerchief, using the clipboard as a table. No one from the ER is watching. It's just Mary and me, and she's convinced I'm just another ER patient who wandered into her room hungry for a good conversation. She's comfortable with me and wants to talk.

"Who are the terrorists, Mary?"

"My husband and the police."

Concern for terrorism is real. I frequently worry about terrorist activity and car bombs. I live on the East Coast, and it's not out of the question that with all the unpatrolled miles of sand and pine forests, some boat could come to shore at midnight and a band of gunslingers would take over the local police department without anyone knowing.

I feel a civic duty well up inside me like a bad fart. I had better continue the conversation just in case Mary has vital information to share.

"Really? That sucks, Mary. Does anyone else know the police are actually terrorists in disguise?"

"I've told a few people, but no one believes me."

"So your husband is a terrorist?"

"He's a retired police officer."

"Why are all these people terrorizing you, Mary?"

"Because I own a lot of land, and my husband wants the money. If he can prove I'm crazy, he will get the deeds."

I take a slow deep breath. Her alibi isn't so crazy after all. An acre of land around here can be worth a million dollars. IVC papers frequently involve disgruntled family members.

"Where is your husband now?"

"At home waiting."

Twenty minutes later Mary and I are still volleying questions and answers back and forth. Her story is detailed and thorough. Everything points to conspiracy and harassment by the husband and his old friends on the police force. I'm getting frustrated because I'm going to be the only one who believes her. Dr. Lowder won't be happy when I recommend that she be transferred to police protection in another county.

Suddenly, I stand up. "Hold that thought, Mary. I hear a phone ringing." I leave the room and go to the nurses' station. Sarah is sitting with CJ and they both grin at me as I lean on the counter.

"Looks like you've made a new friend," Sarah quips.

I shake my head. "I can't punch a good hole in her story."

"The one about her husband?" CJ asks.

"Yeah," I reply with a sigh.

"Maybe it's because you're as crazy as she is," Sarah adds.

I pause. "What's that have to do with anything?"

"You really think she's telling the truth?" CJ is a little surprised at my response.

I think carefully, then reply. "No, I don't. But I still haven't found a flaw in her story. There's a difference."

Silence falls on the three of us as the doors to the ambulance bay slide open. Another patient arrives, seated on a gurney, breathing oxygen, flanked by two paramedics.

"Chest pain," one of them announces casually.

Sarah stands up and points, "Room Two!" She walks around the counter and gets close to me. "I wouldn't have your job, and by the way, you still look like shit."

"Thanks," I manage. "I think you've told me that already."

"When was the last time you ate something healthy?"

"Does Milwaukee's Best count?"

"No. And neither does pizza."

"I'm not sure," I reply sincerely.

"You still have diarrhea?"

"I'm wide open."

"You probably need an IV."

"Seriously?"

"I'll talk to Dr. Lowder." She turns to go.

"Wait!" I'm confused. The only way I'll get through the night is if it's slow, and the ER is already busy with medical and trauma. It's just a matter of time before a wave of mental illness roars through the community. It's a three-day weekend, and the weather has been unusually hot and dry.

"Okay," I finally give in to the idea.

Suddenly I feel naked. I look down and my clothes are in a pile on the floor. I'm exposed, vulnerable. My testicles are shrinking. I go to great lengths to maintain a professional appearance at the ER. I don't share much personal information. I do my job with a smile. I don't fraternize with anyone off duty. Now I'm nude, and everyone is going to know I have diarrhea.

I run into Mary's room and hide in the corner. I'm sweating profusely and out of breath. She's watching me closely. I sit down on the chair and cover my genitals with the clipboard. Bugs are starting to crawl on the walls. I suppress an urge to scratch myself head to toe.

"Are you okay?" Mary asks.

Who's the patient now? Psychotic meltdowns are common. Totally sane one minute and the next insane because a torturous, deeply rooted fear suddenly works its way to the surface.

"I'm fine, Mary. Thanks. It's just...well, I guess we are all in this together, right?"

She looks comfortable with my answer. Mary is ready to continue talking. She knows anything she tells me won't ever leave the room. I'm just another patient waiting for an IV lithium drip.

"Mary, are you suicidal? I mean, do you want to hurt yourself?"

"Gosh, no! I just want help with my husband and the police."

I lean forward and check the ER for Dr. Lowder. I see him tiptoeing into a trauma room, donning rubber gloves, preparing for my rectal exam. Nurses are gathering.

Mary's story is good, but something about the arsenic poisoning she mentioned isn't settling with me. I need to keep moving. I've spent enough time with Mary. People are going to suspect something.

"Mary, tell me again about the arsenic poisoning. Why do you think your husband was trying to poison you with arsenic?"

Delusional thinking runs deep. Delusional thoughts aren't just incorrect thoughts that need to be corrected. Delusions are beliefs, passionate personal decisions about reality and your role in the world. Delusions can alter the human race. Just look at Hitler.

"I gained a hundred and forty-eight pounds in six weeks."

I take a deep breath and flatulate at the same time. I finally found a flaw in her highly developed delusion. Mary weighs about 150 pounds. No one her size could gain 148 pounds in a matter of weeks.

"Mary, I'll see what I can do. I'll talk to Dr. Lowder."

Back in the chart room, I'm on the phone trying to find a psychiatrist who will accept care for Mary. She's an interesting case, so it won't be hard to find her a bed. The more bizarre your story is, the more likely you will be treated. Routine suicidal feelings won't get you anywhere.

Shelly is listening to Rascal Flats again, and I'm ready for some sleep. I consider sneaking through the ER to my quiet hospital bed at the end of the hall, but someone might see me. If I hide in the dark long enough, they will forget about me and just assume I went home.

"You've got another one!" Shelly calls out.

His name is Brad and he's 35 years old. Another IVC taken out by a family member, but this time everyone is in the lobby waiting to talk to me. Brad apparently shot a hole in the wall at home with a shotgun, a .410 to be exact. I own a .410 shotgun, so I'm interested to see what Brad was shooting at. It's a small shotgun used mostly for reducing the squirrel population, but the sound it would make if discharged inside would be incredible. I'm sure Brad's ears are still ringing.

"Can you hear me?" I ask.

Brad blinks a few times and looks at me. "Sure."

Brad is still wearing his clothes, which means the nurses aren't sure what to do with him yet. Dr. Lowder heard his story and quickly passed him on to me. Brad is a little unusual because he ostensibly was threatening to kill someone. That makes him actively homicidal, and that's a crime in most places. What got him to the ER was a history of schizophrenia. He still might go to jail before the night is over.

"What were you hunting?"

I'm not trying to be funny. I want to see if he can recall the events that brought him to the ER. I want to see if he remembers shooting the shotgun.

"I'm being watched."

"By who?"

"The government."

Another conspiracy theory. Conspiracy theories are common and relatively easy to formulate. Just add some paranoia to a delusion of grandeur. It's human nature to want to feel special. If the government is secretly watching you, then you are pretty important.

"What's that have to do with hunting?"

Brad folds his arms, hugging himself, and assumes a defensive posture. He knows why he's at the ER with a sheriff's deputy guarding him, and he's fully aware that he discharged a shotgun into the entertainment center at home. But I'm not here to accuse anyone of wrongdoing. I decide to return to his delusion.

"Someone else tonight mentioned being watched by the government. Why do you think you are being watched?"

I have to gain Brad's trust back. Justifying his feelings is a start. I just suggested he's not alone and something needs to be done about the government.

"The government installed cameras in my house."

"That really sucks, Brad. How do you know they installed cameras?"

"Because I found one."

It was probably his dad's Nikon camera.

"How long have they been watching you?"

Brad relaxes and looks at me sitting in the chair, fiddling with my glasses. I have a bandage wrapped around the hinge as if they are ready to fall apart. Transparent tape doesn't have any effect. I squeeze the bandage so it doesn't fall off.

Brad sighs as if I'm an idiot for not knowing. "A long time!"

I look up and squint, then put my glasses back on.

"Your chart says you are schizophrenic. Is that true?"

"No. They made that up."

"Do you ever hear voices, but you can't find out where they are coming from?"

"All the goddamn time! I look, but I can't find them."

"But you aren't receiving commands or instructions from anyone, right?"

Brad has to think about that one. Auditory hallucinations that involve receiving orders are just plain scary to me. I worry about the day a voice suddenly tells me to pull my teeth out with a pair of pliers.

"No, not commands, but Jesus talks to me regularly."

A conspiracy theory mixed with a religious conviction. Brad is one step away from detonating a pipe bomb in a crowded church.

"That's special, Brad."

Why Brad is being watched by the government and singled out by Jesus doesn't matter any longer. The more I probe the more the schizophrenia will present. Schizophrenics can be very creative.

"Brad, I'll talk to Dr. Lowder, and see if the police know anything about the government installing cameras around here. I'm sure it's illegal. It's against the Constitution, right?"

"Damn right!" Brad points his finger in the air.

"One more thing, Brad. Do you drink alcohol?"

"I like to drink whiskey."

"How much do you drink?"

"A few drinks a day."

Brad's blood alcohol was .200 and he tested positive for cocaine. In addition to taking prescription medication, Brad is self-medicating and shooting guns in the house. No wonder his family is tired of him.

Back in the chart room, I'm burning up the phone lines trying to find empty beds at the psychiatric hospitals. I'm keeping good notes in case I pass out in the bathroom. Sarah threw me a wicked smile across the ER, so I guess that means she talked to Dr. Lowder about my diarrhea. She's a vampire thirsting for my blood.

❊ ❊ ❊

I read her birth date three times just to be sure. Dakota is 12 years old. Her mother took out an IVC for good reason. Dakota stole her car and drove over 150 miles to see her boyfriend. She also took her grandmother's Valium prescription. She admitted to taking the pills three times a day for nervousness. I decide to talk to her mother first, for liability reasons if nothing else. I go to the family room for the interview and put my feet up on a leather foot stool. I don't have a foot stool at my condominium. I've never owned a foot stool. Dakota's mother looks guilty and concerned at the same time.

"I would guess Dakota is smart," I start the conversation.

"She's very smart."

"But does she get good grades?"

"She gets a lot of Cs."

Not surprising. A 12-year-old that can successfully drive 150 miles without an accident or arrest. She went to Wilmington and back. It's a tough drive with lots of traffic, lane changes, lights, and speed zones. I have trouble doing it. And the whole time she was under the influence of Valium.

"I understand that Dakota's behavior isn't acceptable. It's illegal in some ways, but what do you want us to do?"

She looks surprised.

"In other words, if you want us to send her to a mental hospital to be locked up and medicated, it's probably not going to happen."

"I just want her to get some help."

"Is she seeing a therapist?"

"Yes. Dr. Griffin sees her regularly."

"And what does he say?"

"He thinks she is bipolar, but he hasn't given a formal diagnosis."

The psychiatrist is either milking Mom's wallet or confused by Dakota's age. On the other hand, I've read that a bipolar diagnosis should not be given to anyone younger than 16. There are too many hormones involved.

"I'll talk to her, but the best course of action is to see Dr. Griffin as soon as possible, probably Tuesday since tomorrow is a holiday."

She stares at the floor and appears saddened by the conversation. Dumping her delinquent child on us isn't going to work. What should she do with her now? Maybe Grandma will adopt her.

"If you knew how many suicidal patients we have right now, you would understand better. The hospitals are full. Dakota needs a good direction. She needs some understanding. Not understanding from you, but some wisdom about life."

I'm suddenly exhausted by my own words. What the hell am I babbling about? Life, wisdom, understanding? I don't know shit about any of these subjects.

She stands up and smooths out the wrinkles on her slacks. I'm too tired to move. I'm fully reclined in the leather chair, hugging my clipboard.

"Thank you, Dr. Stewart."

"I'll talk to her. But don't be surprised if you drive her home tonight."

The door closes, and I'm alone. I need to get a PhD, so I can get paid more. The job would be the same. Maybe I could enroll in one of those online programs out of Puerto Rico. My eyelids grow heavy, and soon I am sound asleep.

NINE

I hear the door open. I blink my eyes and see a woman silhouetted by a flood of crimson light. She walks into the family room, closing the door behind. The only light in the room is coming from one of the expensive lamps sitting on an expensive end table. I'm still reclined in the leather chair with my feet propped up on the foot stool. I'm hugging my clipboard, and my eyes are struggling to see who it is.

She moves closer. It's Dakota's mom. Her eyes are full of lust and her hands begin to unbutton my shirt. I throw the clipboard against the wall.

"What the hell are you doing?"

I sit up. Sarah is standing in the doorway.

"I think I was sleeping."

"You are a mess!"

"I only wish I felt that good." I stand up and look at my watch. It's 10:00 PM.

"How long have you been in here?"

"About forty-five minutes." I try to straighten my hair.

"We've been looking for you. You have four patients out here!"

"Four?" I feel my knees trembling.

"I want to see you in Room Two right now!"

Nurses are good at giving orders.

"But I forgot the bottle of wine, Sarah."

"Room Two now! You need an IV stat before you pass out."

"Okay. Okay." I hold my hands up in surrender. "Just please don't make a scene. I have a questionable reputation to maintain around here."

"Don't mess with me." She points a finger at me then leaves the room. The long arm of the ER has just slapped me across the face. I'm alone again. I consider hiding from her, but it would be too hard. The family room only has two exits. Sarah is watching one door and Shelly is watching the other.

I take off my glasses and examine my reflection. I look ghostly.

"Four patients," I mumble.

After a quick review of the charts, avoiding any conversation, I go to Room 2. Dakota is one of the four patients in need of a recommendation. Doctors always make people wait, so it's not a problem that they have to wait a little while for me to show up. I'm sweating and disoriented when Sarah comes in.

"Put this gown on."

"Sarah, I'm still working. I can't get undressed."

"Dr. Lowder needs to do a rectal exam, and I need a stool sample to send to the lab." She puts the gown on the bed.

I stare at the floor, wiping my forehead with my handkerchief.

"This is a little more than I expected, Sarah. I just wanted some meds for my diarrhea."

"It's standard procedure. Just do it." I hear some empathy in her voice. Being poked and prodded is a highly unusual event for most people. My anxiety begins to grow exponentially.

A few minutes later, I'm sitting on the bed holding my stool sample. I'm in the gown, but I only took my dress shirt off. I have to get back to work. No one else in the entire county is available to finish my shift. Something moves in the plastic cup. I hold it to the light. It's a worm. Not one, but the sample is infested with parasites. Little red worms are crawling everywhere.

Suddenly, the door flies open and Dr. Lowder and Sarah enter, singing "Happy Birthday" and waving surgical instruments in the air. Three deputies hold me down while I'm tied to the bed. My clothing comes off, and Dr. Lowder grabs hold of my testicles. Sarah hands him a scalpel. CJ and the other nurses lean in the door laughing. I'm about to be castrated.

"This won't hurt much!" he announces.

"But it's only diarrhea!" I scream.

"You are such a baby," Sarah says casually.

I look down at my arm and watch the needle go into the vein. I'm still on my back, but I'm not restrained. It's just the two of us in the room. I still have my clothes on. My testicles are safe for now.

"Dr. Lowder told me to give you two liters of normal saline and a banana bag piggyback. He will be in shortly. You are very dehydrated."

"That's for sure," I whisper.

Dr. Lowder enters the room and puts on sterile gloves. "Sarah says you aren't feeling well."

"That's putting it mildly, Doc."

"Nausea? Vomiting?"

I think for a moment as I watch the IV fluid begin dripping into my veins. "No. Just intense diarrhea for the last three or four days."

"How many BMs are you having?"

"I've lost count really, Doc."

He examines the stool sample. "I would guess there's some blood in this. Not unusual if your colon is irritated. We'll send this to the lab. I'll need to do a rectal exam. Drop your pants and lie on your side. In the meantime, I ordered some IV fluids for you."

Sarah takes the stool sample and closes the door. I take a deep breath and assume the position. Thank God Dr. Lowder has small hands.

"Hey Doc, do you know how many people in America are diagnosed with depression?"

"No, I don't."

"About fifteen million, and a lot more are going untreated." I'm trying to create a distraction. "The leading pharmaceutical companies are so frustrated with psychiatric drug development they are shutting down most production. The drugs just don't work at all, or they don't work for very long."

"That's no good."

"Yeah. So, patients soon won't have good meds to take, and self-medication will be a reasonable answer. So will all kinds of experimental treatments like burning holes in your brain and inserting electrodes."

"Can't wait to see that."

"Bipolar is especially hard to treat. A good cocktail of medication may stop working after only a few months."

"You can pull your pants up now."

I sit up and wait for a diagnosis. Dr. Lowder takes off the latex gloves and throws them in the trash.

"It's probably a bacterial invasion of some kind. Finish these fluids, and I will write a prescription for the diarrhea." He opens the door, and a wave of noise and activity floods the room. He looks out, then back at me. Dr. Lowder suddenly appears concerned.

"Are you still working?"

"Until tomorrow at five PM. I feel better already, Doc."

"Good." He disappears into the emergency room chaos.

Sarah comes back in with the second liter of normal saline. She hangs it on the IV pole and adjusts the flow.

"I have to get back to work," I announce.

"You really should just go home."

"Are you kidding? Sarah, I don't have any backup."

"Well, that's just nuts. Your employer needs to get some more people like you."

I laugh. "And how easy would that be?"

Dakota is still waiting for a recommendation and so is Dr. Lowder. I take my clipboard and stand up. "Do you think anyone would notice if I went into Room Four wearing a hospital gown and pushing an IV pole?"

Sarah puts her hands on her hips, looks at me, then at the growing commotion in the ER. "Probably not."

I'm only two rooms away from Dakota. Walking as fast as I can and pushing the four-wheeled, stainless-steel contraption ahead of me, I duck into her room and push the door nearly closed. She's lying in the hospital bed with her arms crossed and looks startled. I have her full and undivided attention.

"Hi, Dakota. I'm Stewart. Dr. Lowder wanted me to talk to you."

"What's wrong with you?"

"I haven't been feeling well."

Dakota sits up full of energy and crosses her legs, ready for a conversation.

I sit down with my IV pole next to me. "Look, I don't want to waste any of your time, so I'll tell you straight up, I've already had a conversation with your mom. Whether anything she told me was true or not, I'm not sure yet. But I think there's no doubt that you drove to Wilmington and back and have a habit of taking your grandmother's medication."

"It's not a habit."

As I suspected, she's smart and pays attention to details.

"Do you know why you are at the ER and not in jail right now? You've broken laws, not bones, right?"

She thinks about the question. It's apparent she wants someone to listen to her concerns. Her mother may not have time or the intelligence to keep up with her mood swings. A smart kid showing signs of bipolar disorder can exhaust the whole family.

"I guess my mom thinks I'm suicidal."

"Exactly. Otherwise, there's no reason for you to be here. You see a psychiatrist here in town?"

"Yes. Dr. Griffin."

"What does he say?"

"He thinks I'm bipolar."

"What do you think?"

"I'm not sure. Maybe I am."

"How would you define bipolar disorder, Dakota?"

"Mood swings?" She's not sure.

"Yes. But very serious mood swings. So high that you don't sleep for days, and so low that you can't get out of bed."

"I don't do that. I'm just tired of babysitting. I have two sisters and a brother, and my mom makes me watch them all week. It makes me depressed. I don't have a life!"

Simple chemistry: if you add pressure, temperature increases. Dysfunctional families are the same. Add pressure to the family, and someone will have a meltdown.

"That sucks, Dakota." I look up at my IV bag. It's almost empty. Two liters of vitamins straight into my veins, I feel like I could outrun a speeding bullet. I just hope the bill isn't too expensive. I don't have any insurance. Maybe Dr. Lowder won't charge me a dime because I'm a trusted colleague.

I stand up and support myself with the IV pole. "You have good reason to be mad, Dakota. Just quit taking your grandmother's Valium and don't drive unless you have a license. You are only twelve."

"Okay." Her answer appears genuine.

"I have to go now. I have three more people to see."

"I hope you feel better, Stewart."

"Thank you."

Only a nice kid would care enough to say such a thing. Most adults would be thinking if they could sue the hospital for having to endure such unprofessional treatment.

It's nearing midnight and the IV fluids made me hungry. I just inhaled some lukewarm pizza and a gallon of Coke from the break room. Dr. Lowder gave me some magic pink pills for the diarrhea, and the IV pole went to the next patient. I'm just hoping I won't have to run to the bathroom again.

Three patients are waiting, so I get busy. Under these circumstances, quick and pointed conversations are best. Are you going to be a liability to the hospital if we send you home, or are you going to take up a bed the entire night waiting for a mental hospital to accept you? You want to sober up now after ten years of abusing yourself? Go home and try it on your own. Come back another day, preferably between 8 and 5.

Charles is 78 years old. His family is concerned he can't take care of himself any longer. They called 911 and initiated a chain of events that won't stop. Emergency medicine is relentless.

"Why in the hell did this guy have to come in at midnight?" I ask Sarah in passing.

"You must be feeling better!"

I knock on the open door and enter his room. Charles is nicely dressed and animated. He sits up and quickly extends his hand for a warm handshake. He appears healthy and probably feels a lot better than I do.

"What can I help you with, Doctor?"

"Just a few questions, Charles."

"Okay. Shoot!"

"Well, do you know where you are?"

"Yes! The hospital. This is the emergency room." He is full of smiles.

"Good, Charles." I start drawing a picture of a Milwaukee's Best beer can. Charles thinks I'm taking careful notes. "Do you know why you are here?"

He's still sitting on the edge of the bed. "Well, Doctor, not really." The smile washes from his face. He looks like a man who wants an answer.

"Charles, your family is concerned about you."

"Why are they concerned, Doctor?"

I turn a page on my clipboard and pretend to read. "You drove to Myrtle Beach without telling your family, and you were found on the beach talking to yourself. Then you were taken to a local hospital."

"That was yesterday!" He smiles again, remembering the day, and pokes the air with his finger.

I'm about to change my line of questioning when he adds, "I took a vacation with some spirits!"

"Really?" Now he has my full attention. "What kind of spirits?"

"Two females, twenty-something."

I sit back in the chair. What's the possibility he picked up two hitchhikers or met two girls on the beach? Charles is a smiley likable guy. I can see a couple of girls wanting to hang out with him, wanting to spend time with a grandfather that's fun and full of life.

"That sounds like fun, Charles. I guess the problem is your family. Why are they so concerned?"

He puts the memory away and grows serious. "They say I might have dementia." He looks at me through thick glasses. "Old-timer's disease."

"Alzheimer's disease?"

"Yes."

Charles became combative with the police in Myrtle Beach and with his family after returning home. He was handcuffed and arrested in Myrtle Beach. Charges of resisting an officer are still pending.

"Charles, do you live alone?"

"Yes, I do."

"So do I. Maybe it wouldn't hurt if you got a roommate. Someone to keep you company?"

"Well, I guess I could do that. Sure, Doctor." He forces a smile.

"I'll see what I can do, Charles."

Charles isn't suicidal. He's not homicidal. He has some dementia, but not enough to warrant further incarceration. I couldn't be so lucky to hang out with two young girls, whether real or imagined. After talking to his concerned family in the lobby and discussing IVC proceedings, they decided to pack up and take him home. My advice to them was assisted living, and to ask for a young nurse to look after him. His wife had died fifteen years ago.

Allen is 33 and he smoked four hundred dollars' worth of crack cocaine, hoping to have a heart attack.

"Hey CJ, how many people can get high on four hundred dollars of crack cocaine?"

"I should know this." She's rubbing her temples trying to do the math. "You said four people per gram, so sixteen people!"

Sarah and Linda laugh. We are taking a micro break at the nurses' station. The ER is starting to look like a three-ring circus with wild animals loose everywhere, and all we have are clipboards and syringes to defend ourselves.

"EMS is bringing in a guy who tried to jump off the intracoastal bridge," CJ says, hanging up the phone.

"Wow," I respond. "That would have killed him for sure. It's not very deep below the bridge, but it's a hell of a long way down. Lots of oyster beds and fast currents. I fish there sometimes."

I look over and see Dr. Mattia has started his shift. Dr. Lowder is busy talking on the phone, dictating his notes so he can go home.

The nursing staff will change in the morning. I'm done when the sun rises, sails across the blue sky, and starts setting again.

I go back to Allen's room. He doesn't look like he wants to talk. He's still high on cocaine and probably starting to come down. His girlfriend found him trying to hang himself, and that was no more than forty-five minutes ago, thanks to an efficient 911 system.

"Why did you try to hang yourself, Allen?"

"Fuck you!"

I sit back in my chair and slide my glasses up my nose. Allen will obviously need further psychiatric support and pharmaceutical intervention, starting with a ten-day cocktail of psychotropic medications to numb his brain. Allen needs an attitude adjustment. I could stop the interview right now, but I'm feeling good. It's always a challenge to pry open someone's mind.

"You apparently tied a working noose, which takes practice. What were you going to hang yourself from? That's usually the problem when trying to hang yourself. Everything breaks and you fall on the floor pissed off with a rope around your neck."

Allen looks at me like he wants to kill me. The door is open and a deputy sheriff is at the nurses' station. He is drinking coffee, talking to the nurses, and watching our conversation closely.

Suicide and homicide become one and the same when you are desperate to die. People that get in your way are expendable.

"The fucking rafters in the garage."

It's my job to establish a safe plan for outpatient treatment. If I can't determine the patient will be safe being released to their family to go home and sleep it off, then I get on the phone and find them a mental hospital where they will be locked up and watched closely.

Silence is a truth serum. Allen breaks the silence with additional information that he probably didn't want to share.

"I'm having financial problems and problems with my girlfriend. I've been depressed my whole fucking life. All these medications the doctors prescribe me don't do shit!"

Allen crosses his arms. He is feeling vulnerable. "Do you know what it's like being depressed all the time?"

"I know what it's like being depressed, Allen. Nothing tastes good. Nothing feels good. Smiling and laughing are a waste of time. It makes you want to kill people who seem to have it together."

I finally got his attention. He looks down at me sitting in the chair, fidgeting. Hospital beds are always elevated.

"Yeah. I don't even want to have sex."

"Look, Allen." I stand up. "We can't send you home like this. You will need more support than we can offer here."

"Like a mental hospital?"

"Yes. But one thing to remember." Good advice sometimes sounds cheap and poorly rehearsed. I hesitate but decide to continue. "Suicide is a permanent solution to a temporary problem."

With that I quickly exit the room and head for the phones. It was a quote from a psychology book that always made good sense to me. Allen may or may not have heard me.

As I pass by Dr. Mattia, I see a five-second window to share my current recommendations. He is standing next to his desk and reading a chart.

"Hey Doc, the cocaine abuser is actively suicidal. I can't develop a safe outpatient plan with him. I'll get on the phone and find him a bed somewhere. The kid in Room Four is just rebellious. She's not suicidal. Her mom agrees to take her home. The guy shooting shotguns in the house is highly delusional and needs serious help and so does the lady crying conspiracy theory. She's not suicidal and might have to go home if I can't transfer her."

He nods his head and turns to the trauma room. Someone needs a wound cleaned and sutured.

"Doc?"

"Yes, Stewart." He looks at me.

"I know you want to move these psych patients out of here, but beds are going to be hard to find tonight."

He nods his head again and walks away. My point had a double meaning. First, I was saying don't be surprised if you have to send some of these mental patients home, and second, don't be pissed at me if I don't try too hard to transfer them. I know better than anyone how full the psychiatric units are and how uncaring the mental health system can be when it gets busy.

I look at the message board on the wall to see who is next. It's a computer-driven flat screen that summarizes the patient's name, the nurse assigned, and the patient status, among other things. The information is color coded and fairly detailed. I frequently find myself standing in the middle of the ER staring at the electronic data, trying to determine how much longer I have until I can go home. Red means the patient is waiting for tests or an assessment. PSY means psychiatric, which means me.

I'm feeling superhuman with two extra liters of IV fluid running through my veins; however, the vitamin-fortified fluid is beginning to soak into the dehydrated tissues. My high is wearing off. What I really need is a real meal and a 6-pack of beer. I'll be sure to motivate

Leroy to go out to dinner tonight. It's 1:30 AM; dinner is sixteen hours away. I can make it through the 72-hour shift if I can get a few hours of sleep. Suddenly, I hear a patient scream. It's one of mine.

"Hey, Linda." I grab her elbow as she walks by. Linda is the youngest and most attractive nurse on the ER staff. She has long brown hair and a shapely figure. As I make a great effort to hide from the hospital when I'm not working, I know little about her. I've been meaning to ask her out to dinner or to share a 12-pack of beer and some free golf.

"Is that your patient that just screamed?"

She turns and faces me with impeccable posture. I imagine Fred Astaire meeting Ginger Rogers but suffering diarrhea and waiting for his black-tie world to flush away. I'm instantly intimidated. Everyone is watching.

"Yes, it is. He suffered a gunshot wound to the head seven months ago, poor thing."

She's sweet. She's compassionate. She's seemingly immune to the toxicity of the ER. I want to ask her if she would like to meet me in the Fast Track in my private room so we could spoon for a while on the electric hospital bed and watch the LED lights on the artificial life-support equipment blink on and off.

"I'll talk to him and let you know if I find anything interesting." I'm about to go when I surprise myself and ask, "Maybe we could go out sometime. I live on a golf course if you like to play golf."

She lowers her head and looks at the floor for a moment. I feel the burning sting of rejection is about to slap my face. She looks up at me with a big smile and nearly laughs. I'm completely confused.

"I would love to…but I'm pregnant."

Some answers are hard to respond to. Linda just gave me too much information, but at the same time, she set some clear boundaries. She didn't say yes, and she didn't say no. She said ordinary sex is out of the question, and she said if I spend too much time with her, I'll be changing diapers. She didn't say she had a boyfriend or a significant other. Maybe she got knocked up at a bar, drunk, on a pool table, during a tournament.

"Wow. That's great. Congratulations!" is all I can think of.

I can hardly wait to have a normal conversation with another mental patient, as I hurry away to interview the screaming man.

TEN

"What's going on here?"

Sarah and David, one of the few male nurses on the ER staff, are trying to get the patient into a hospital gown. They are letting him keep his pants on, but getting his shirt off is essential for doing examinations and administering IV fluids and taking blood samples. Removing a patient's pants means they aren't going home anytime soon.

Sarah and David ignore me, but the screaming man looks up. His name is Peter and he is 41 years old. He yells again. But it's not a scream, just a loud response to being manipulated like a puppet on strings. He thinks I'm somebody special with a clipboard and glasses.

"I came here for help, not to get my clothes stolen off my back!" he complains.

Sarah throws her hands in the air and leaves the room. "He's all yours!"

"They just need to get you in a gown, Peter. Everyone here wears a gown."

"What the hell for?"

"So you don't make a mess of your own clothes if you eat something."

David puts a blood pressure cuff on Peter's arm and pumps it up. Peter is distracted for a moment, then adds, "Well, I'm not hungry!"

I sit down and attempt to blend into the wall, posing as little of a threat as possible. David gets finished with vitals and leaves the room. Peter rubs his arm and looks around the room for his clothes.

"Peter, you came in voluntarily. Why are you here?"

Peter continues to rub away the pain of the blood pressure cuff and searches his memory for a reasonable answer. The gunshot wound was to his head and it happened seven months ago. A simple concussion can cause memory loss for several months. A piece of lead traveling at 1,000 feet per second, punching a hole in the skull, then traumatizing the brain like a bowling ball blasting through helpless pins—it's a wonder people survive GSWs to the head.

"I was worried I was going to hurt myself or maybe someone else."

"How were you going to hurt yourself, Peter?"

"I don't know. Probably cut my wrists. If you let me go, I'll do it in the parking lot before you have a chance to stop me!"

I hear more screaming but it's coming from the ER. Peter and I both pause to watch EMS bringing in the jumper. He is handcuffed to the gurney and flanked by two police officers. He's a 20-something male, and I can see his eyes are rolled up in his head, and he is foaming at the mouth.

I'm suddenly bored with Peter's suicidal ideations. Peter must be a frequent flyer somewhere because words like that can buy you psychiatric treatment for at least forty-eight hours. Maybe he's hiding from someone.

"I don't even know why I'm here," he adds.

"You just said you were suicidal, Peter."

"No. I mean I live in Mississippi. I don't know how I got to North Carolina." He appears confused and frustrated. "Since I got shot, I've had terrible headaches, and I get confused easily."

"Do you have family here?" I'm still considering sending him home. Until we see knife cuts on the wrists, no one is going to care too much.

"I think about killing people. I even set a car on fire last week. I was mad at someone. It burnt to the ground."

I look away from the ER and stare at Peter. He appears genuinely sorrowful.

"You set a car on fire?"

"I was mad."

"Do the police know?"

"I didn't get caught."

I think about my yellow Jeep. As much as I don't like it, I would be pissed off if someone set it on fire.

"Peter, that's not…"

I'm at a loss for words. I was going to say not legal or not nice. If I find the time, I will tell one of the deputies about his confession. On the other hand, one less car in the world won't hurt anything. It might help the environment.

❁ ❁ ❁

I'm intrigued by the patient foaming at the mouth, so I excuse myself and leave Peter's room. I meet CJ as she is exiting the examination room. I look over her shoulder and watch him convulse in the bed like he is having a seizure. But it's not a seizure. He is mumbling something, and the whites of his eyes are the only thing showing.

"Is he rabid?"

"I need a cigarette." CJ is clearly upset. She has supplies for a blood draw in her hands, but the patient doesn't have an IV.

He raises his voice. It's a foreign language. He growls, then actually hisses like a snake. The two deputies by his bed take a step back. He is now four-pointed to the hospital bed with cloth restraints. EMS needed their gurney back, and the deputies won't give up their handcuffs for long. The paramedics are quick to leave the ER. There's a head-on collision somewhere nearby. A helicopter is enroute. I glance at Dr. Mattia. He's an iceman. No emotions are visible. He is juggling charts, giving orders, and entering notes as fast as he can. Fortunately, the staff is highly trained. The nurses can take care of themselves.

"Is he possessed?" I'm dumbfounded.

"Apparently so," CJ replies.

"I say we give him a little Ativan and send him home then."

"I agree!" She pats herself down looking for cigarettes.

"CJ, what are we supposed to do with demon possession? This isn't a church."

She smiles. "You figure it out."

His name is Ronald, and he is 26 years old. Local police found him standing on the Intracoastal Waterway bridge, ready to jump into the water 120 feet below. They make the bridges tall to accommodate big sailboats. He was speaking a foreign language and acting in a bizarre manner. I stand next to his bed and watch him tugging on the restraints, writhing like a wild animal. His pupils are still rolled up in his head, and the foaming has stopped for the moment.

"Ronald, can you hear me?"

David comes into the room to draw blood. It's possible Ronald is high on drugs. It's even possible he's suffering from a medical condition. Ronald turns his head toward me and hisses. I take a step back.

"I'll take that as a yes."

He tugs at the restraints again. Restraining a patient is unusual in an emergency room. Law enforcement restrains people who are a threat to persons or property. Cops carry handcuffs. ERs have nice soft cloth strips, which require numerous people at the same time to tie someone down.

Ronald whispers something to me. I take a step closer. David distracts him by tying a tourniquet around his arm.

"Belias!" he hisses at David.

"He's been repeating that word." David casually sticks Ronald with a needle and draws a blood sample for the lab. "I'm going to go online and look it up."

David finishes and leaves me with Ronald. I take a deep breath and stand next to his bed, holding on to the stainless steel siderail he's tied to. I've seen a lot of delusional patients. Most of them are crying conspiracy theories. The government is after them. Cameras are hidden in the bathroom. My television is watching me!

I silently watch Ronald slithering on the bed, hissing quietly, turning his head back and forth. He has yet to look at anyone, so I haven't seen his pupils. It's disturbing to me that all I can see is the white sclera. Lots of horror movies capitalize on that same special effect.

"Who is Belias, Ronald?"

"My father," he manages. Ronald's voice is different now. His response appears to be sincere. It seems he is willing to answer some questions.

"Do you know why you are here at the Emergency Room, Ronald?"

"I tried to kill myself."

"Right. And we don't want you to do that." I'm not really sure if it would matter. A lot of people wouldn't be missed if they would jump off a bridge into fast-moving current—more fish food.

Ronald responds to my kindness by hissing loudly and tugging at the restraints. I must have hit a nerve. Sarah comes through the door with a syringe.

"Ronald, Dr. Mattia ordered some medication."

She wastes no time and injects him in the arm. Ronald hisses again.

"Are you two getting to be friends?" she asks, waving the syringe in my face.

"What was that?"

"A sedative."

"I'll come back in a little while then."

The interview wasn't going to be very productive anyhow. Altering a patient's level of consciousness can sometimes open up a good discussion, as long as they don't fall asleep.

I leave Ronald's room and go to the nurse's station to reevaluate my strategy. New patients are coming in by the minute. I'm gripped with anxiety. I have enough work in front of me for three people. I look at my watch. It's 2:30 AM. The only good news I can think of is Ronald will be easy to transfer. He's an interesting patient, at the very least, and mental hospitals like bizarre patients. The psychiatrists get bored. I decide juggling everyone at once is the best solution. If no one goes home and kills themselves in the next twenty-four hours, I will consider my 72-hour shift a success.

❊ ❊ ❊

Her name is Linda and she's 39 years old. She was admitted for a possible intentional overdose of cocaine. She told Dr. Mattia she doesn't need counseling, detox, or any help, and just wants to go home.

"Linda, my name is Stewart. Dr. Mattia wants me to talk to you to see if we can send you home safely."

The nurses put Linda in a gown and she's sitting on the bed hugging her knees. She's guarded but appears alert and oriented. Lab blood work showed no alcohol. Urine drug screen showed a positive for cocaine only.

"I'm fine. I just want to go home."

"I appreciate that, but we just want to make sure you have a safe plan, so you don't leave here and kill yourself."

She looks me in the eye and presses her response. "I'm not suicidal!"

"You just did too much cocaine, right?"

She's hiding something. "Well, sort of."

"Linda, I can't recommend releasing you until you come clean with me."

She squirms, then leans toward me and whispers, "I'm working undercover."

"Really?" I'm skeptical.

"I'm working with the Sheriff Department."

"Doing what?"

"I'm working undercover as a drug dealer."

"Well, that's interesting, but a good drug dealer doesn't do drugs."

A successful drug dealer stays sober so they can focus on trafficking merchandise. Purchasing, distribution, and sales are hard enough with the entire operation being illegal and hidden at all times.

"Okay, so I messed up. I was making a deal and snorted some of it, so I wouldn't look like a narc."

Not a bad story. As long as she's not suicidal, I really don't care.

"Then how much did you snort?"

"A lot! Enough to get me here. I thought my heart was going to explode."

"So you called nine-one-one?"

"Yes. After I finished the deal and went home."

"Where are the deputies you are working with?"

A normal drug bust would happen as soon as the money exchanged hands. Linda shouldn't be sitting here talking to me. She should be under arrest and waiting for her law enforcement friends to release her without any charges.

She thinks for a long moment. "I'm not sure."

"Well, your story doesn't make much sense." I stand up and tuck my clipboard under my arm, ready to leave. "You aren't having a heart attack, Linda. And if you are abusing cocaine, you need to stop. I'll talk to Dr. Mattia and see if we can send you home." I turn and make eye contact with her. I'm standing in the doorway. I'm giving her one more chance to add any details to her unbelievable story.

"Linda, are you in any danger? I would hate to have a shooting in the ER parking lot."

She shakes her head and swallows hard. "No."

Back to the nurses' station. I do my best to keep them informed of my findings. Typically, they know as much as I do even after I interview a patient. The details frequently don't matter. Are you suicidal right now as we are speaking? No? Then go home and sleep it off. Here, take this Ativan before you sign out.

It's 3:00 AM and I'm feeling pretty run down. My IV therapy was hours ago. I can't remember the last time I had a good meal. I can't recall the last time I ate a fruit or a vegetable. All I eat is break-room pizza and soda when I'm on call. At least my diarrhea has stopped.

I decide to check on Peter to see if his suicidal ideations have cleared up. I'm willing to give him another chance to quit being stupid. Cutting your wrists isn't the best approach to suicide anyhow.

Peter is watching TV when I enter the room. He must have turned it on because it's not standard procedure to let patients watch *I Dream of Jeannie* after admitting to trying to kill themselves.

"Hey, Peter? Do you still want to kill yourself?"

He looks at me like I'm crazy for even asking.

"Give me my damn clothes back! I'm ready to leave."

I have to make tough decisions. I just wish it wasn't 3:00 AM. It's easy to want to clear out the ER to make the staff happy. The faster I can process the mentally ill the better the machine will run. As I said, emergency rooms don't like mental illness.

"Peter, do you own a gun?"

"Hell no!"

I own ten guns. I have an arsenal at home. I'm always amazed when people say they don't own a gun.

"What are you going to do if we release you?"

"Probably go home and have a goddamn drink!"

"Do you know where you live?"

"Hell yes, I know where I live!"

"So, you won't cut your wrists in the parking lot or set any more cars on fire, right?"

He has to think for a moment. "Well, I can't promise anything. But I'm ready to go! I volunteered to come here, and now I'm volunteering to leave. Where are my clothes?"

I wait a long moment to see if he adds anything. Silence fills the room. The chaos from the ER steals across the floor like a deadly fog. I can hear Ronald hissing again, and the sliding glass doors to the ambulance bay opening. Further away I can detect the backing signal from a diesel fire truck, and beyond that I hear CJ's lighter flick in the cool morning air.

Once again, I find myself staring mindlessly at the monitor on the wall. I have another patient that just arrived by ambulance for cocaine abuse. They put him in a trauma room because all the beds are full. Dr. Mattia walks by me, consumed with thought. He looks unusually tired but he's keeping it together.

"A lot of cocaine in this county, Doc."

He stops to consider the thought.

"And why do you think we have so much cocaine here, Stewart?"

I know he has an answer of his own.

"We live on the Atlantic Coast. All the boats that come in and out of here…shoot, law enforcement doesn't stand a chance."

He nods his head in agreement.

I continue, "It's hard to tell who's running drugs. Even the commercial shrimp boats could be dirty."

"And we get to mop up the mess."

For a moment, he's lost in thought, then he walks away and goes into the trauma room. Communicating with the ER doctors isn't easy. Engine-room mechanics probably feel the same when they brush by the captain of the ship. Get out of the way and salute is the best response. The doctors here think I'm a little crazy anyhow. I need to be to get this job done.

❊ ❊ ❊

His name is Thomas, and he's 35 years old. Thomas is lying on one of our trauma beds taking up valuable space. Thomas is positive for cocaine, which isn't surprising since he admitted to smoking crack cocaine for the last six days. Tears are streaming down his cheeks and he's lying on his side in a fetal position looking completely helpless. Thomas is a big man, 6 foot 6 inches tall, and pushing 300 pounds. He looks pathetic, held hostage by an illegal white powder.

"Thomas, my name is Stewart. Dr. Mattia wanted me to talk to you about your cocaine problem."

"I just want to die!" he says through tears and sobbing.

I'm immediately pissed off because Thomas just complicated the interview. He wants help that doesn't exist. Drug abusers need to help themselves. The ER is for emergencies, like heart attacks and gunshot wounds.

I take a long, jagged breath. "How long have you been smoking cocaine, Thomas?"

"A few years. I feel like I'm losing my mind." More sobbing, more tears.

I look around for a chair but there isn't one. An IV pole is next to his bed, and it crosses my mind to beat him with it. I move closer and grip the stainless steel with my free hand. It's cold and sturdy. Thomas won't know what hit him.

"So, you decided to quit your cocaine habit at four o'clock on a Monday morning during a holiday weekend?" I pick the IV pole up and weigh it in my hands.

"I just want to die," he sobs again.

I take a few practice swings, ripping the pole through the stale air. "Hey batter, batter, swing!" I can hear the crowd standing up, applauding, waiting for me to hit a home run with Thomas's head.

Sarah walks into the trauma room. I look down and I'm holding my clipboard and pen. I clear my throat. "I was just about to school Thomas on why it's about impossible to get inpatient help for drug abuse at four AM."

Sarah puts a blood pressure cuff on his arm. "Quit doing cocaine, Thomas," she says casually.

"I can't!" he cries.

Ronald starts hissing again. I can hear him through all the commotion. It's an odd sound, an unfamiliar sound, then I hear a woman scream. EMS has arrived with another patient. I step out of the trauma room to make a quick assessment. White female, late 20s, high on drugs or possibly suffering a manic episode. She's not restrained, not yet.

"Let me go you fucking assholes!"

She's squirming, flailing her arms, and making a scene. EMS is quick to transfer her to the hospital bed and leave. A huddle of nurses runs into the room to tie her to the stainless-steel bedrails.

I look down at my clipboard and write the number three on Thomas's lab report. I have three patients to assess, three patients to make a recommendation on, and three patients to get out of the ER as soon as possible. Dr. Mattia doesn't like his ER filled with mental illness.

I go back into the trauma room to deal with Thomas. I'm not going to transfer him to a detox facility because it's not worth the effort. He needs outpatient support and some new friends.

He is lying on his side trying to fall asleep, still high on cocaine.

"Thomas, wake up." He lifts his head and stares at me with bloodshot eyes.

"Thomas, the solution to your problem is to quit doing cocaine and spend time with people who don't do drugs. You aren't going to suffer much, if any, withdrawal symptoms, so it's just a matter of staying sober. Do you think you can handle that?"

Thomas surprises me and immediately sits up in bed. I must have gotten through to him. I feel a sudden sense of accomplishment.

"I know what I need to do," he mumbles.

"Great! I'll talk to Dr. Mattia, and we will get you discharged as soon as possible." I leave in a hurry and run into Sarah as she is coming into the trauma room.

"Let's get Thomas out of there before he gets stupid."

Sarah stops and takes a deep breath. "Drug abusers make me nuts. Where do they get the money?"

"I've got the money, Sarah, but who has the time? Leroy has been at my house for a week, and I haven't had time to drink with him."

She forces a smile, then goes to take Thomas's vitals again. He holds out his arm indifferently and mechanically. Alcohol withdrawal can kill you. Cocaine withdrawal won't kill you. There is a free clinic across the street from the hospital open 8 to 5, Monday through Friday. Thomas will get a handful of free literature before he leaves and an earful of cheap advice from Dr. Mattia or one of the nurses. Hurry up and leave so we can use your bed for the next patient. People are lined up at the door waiting for quick answers to their emergencies.

ELEVEN

I quietly enter Ronald's room to observe his behavior. His eyes are nearly closed and there's too much noise in the ER for him to have heard me. He is still writhing in the bed, tugging at the restraints, but the sedative they gave him appears to be working. I watch silently, trying to determine if it's an act. Delusions can be powerful. This could be a well-rehearsed presentation used to keep people from hurting him or getting close to him. Some people go as far as defecating themselves to keep people away. I can still see the whites of his eyes glowing from his angry beet-red complexion. I shake my head, wondering.

Peter was discharged with all his clothing. Hopefully he will get out of the parking lot before doing something illegal. Thomas will be discharged momentarily with some expensive words of wisdom to chew on. I hear more profanity from the next room, so I decide to start another assessment. It's my job to keep the mental patients quiet so the ER staff can get their work done.

Her name is Michelle and she is 29 years old. Her family was able to get her to the ER voluntarily without IVC papers, but that can easily change now that we have legal jurisdiction over her. If we determine she is not fit to care for herself, she will lose all her rights. According to the chart, Michelle suffers from bipolar disorder and hasn't slept for five days. She apparently lives alone and decided to quit taking her medication. I'm surprised to read that she visited the ER yesterday but left before seeing the attending physician.

"Michelle, my name is Stewart. Do you know why you are here?"

She is tied to the bedrails and looks at me like I'm from another planet. That makes two mental patients four-pointed to their beds. It's highly unusual to have one patient requiring restraints. Dr. Mattia isn't in the mood to play around tonight.

"Let me go! I need to masturbate!"

Some interviews are weirder than others. I immediately take off my glasses and turn them around to check my reflection. I expect to see myself screaming, but I look calm and collected as usual. Fake it until you make it is my motto.

Did she say masturbate?

Bipolar patients caught in a manic phase are frequently hypersexual. I get propositioned and insulted on a regular basis trying to counsel bipolar women having emotional meltdowns.

"I need to masturbate!" she screams.

Sarah hurries into the room with IV supplies. I'm too tired to say anything witty, so I just get to the point. "Looks like bipolar disorder manic episode noncompliant with medications."

Michelle tugs on her restraints and yells again.

"You need to be quiet! We don't talk like that around here," Sarah says with as much sincerity as possible.

"I'll talk any way I want, bitch!"

Manic episodes can present in many ways. Underlying psychotic features appear to come to the surface as the phase continues. One of two outcomes will occur: the patient will begin a depressive cycle without hurting anyone, or the mania will cause a meltdown of some kind, and they will end up at the ER or in jail. Michelle's drug screen will probably come back positive for numerous recreational drugs. The interview will have to wait until she gets her medication. I'm not in the mood to be propositioned or insulted by anyone.

More phone calls and paperwork, and twenty minutes later I decide to check on Ronald. It's rare that I see a patient complaining of demonic possession. I'm looking forward to interrogating him to see if it's real. If he's faking psychosis, he will cost the local medical community a lot of time and money. I will take an aggressive direct line of questioning if needed. We see people that fake seizures just to get a dose of Valium. I can't let anyone slip through our cracks.

I touch him on the shoulder. "Hey Ronald, wake up. My name is Stewart. Dr. Mattia wanted me to talk to you."

I'm a little nervous, but I stick to the basics. I need to gain Ronald's trust and pose as little a threat as possible. I remain standing next to his bed and rest my clipboard on the bedrail like a shield. If he tries to attack me, I hope the restraints hold. He turns his head toward me and hisses.

"Ronald, tell me again who Belias is."

"My father told me to jump off the bridge." His voice is clear and audible. I sense some genuine remorse.

"Why did you try to jump off the bridge, Ronald?"

He hisses softly, I see only the whites of his eyes. "My father wants me to die."

"Why?"

Ronald is sedated for sure, but he appears oriented enough to answer my questions. David enters the room suddenly. I watch Ronald closely. He turns his head to David without looking at him. His white eyes are disturbing. I can't make my eyes do that. Ronald hisses again.

"I looked up Belias on the internet. It's an ancient name for the devil."

For some reason Ronald lifts his head off the pillow and looks at me. I guess it's my turn to say something.

"So, Belias is the devil. The devil is your father. And he told you to jump off the bridge, right?"

Ronald responds by talking in a foreign language. The words are garbled and hard to distinguish from one another. With my limited exposure to languages other than English, I would guess it's Latin. He writhes in the bed and tugs at his restraints. David draws blood for the lab, and Ronald is surprisingly calm.

"Ronald, do you want to kill yourself?"

The patient has a dramatic presentation, yes. However, it's always my job to determine if they are homicidal or suicidal, and can we send them home after a good dose of psychotropic medication to avoid clogging up the mental health system. More than anything, at this point, after witnessing hundreds of people dancing with the devil, suffering psychological meltdowns, working in this ER for the last three years as a crisis counselor, I just want to know if Ronald is really possessed by a demon.

"Ronald, answer me, do you want to die?" I raise my voice and lean closer.

"No," he whispers. His voice changes again. He appears to have two distinct personalities. I decide to use a different line of questioning. I make the assumption that Ronald is being honest.

"How long have you been possessed by the devil?"

"Belias!" he hisses.

"Let me guess, Ronald. You've had this problem all your life, right?"

I consider the difficulty of having such an affliction. How could you make friends or engage in a meaningful relationship? Ronald has surely been alone most of his life.

"A root," he whispers.

"A what?"

"A root is a curse," David replies.

"Ronald, who gave you this curse?" I worry for a moment that his unpleasant curse might get in my head and make me drive my Jeep off a bridge.

"Grandmother," he hisses softly.

"Your grandmother put a curse on you?" And I thought my family was crazy. My parents gave me issues, but I don't think anyone has ever put a curse on me.

"She put it on the whole family," he whispers.

Grandma may have had issues, too. That's just not nice. My grandmother fed me banana nut cupcakes and smiled a lot. Ronald or the devil, I'm not sure which, quickly grows tired of my questions. He hisses loudly and writhes in the bed, tugging violently on the cloth restraints.

I hear the sliding doors to the ambulance bay, then a man yelling. My interview with Ronald is over. I leave the room and look to see who my next patient is. To my amazement, it's Thomas, returning on a gurney, crying hysterically and slobbering all over himself. Dr. Mattia is standing by the nurses' station with his hands on his hips, looking irritated. Sarah steers the gurney back into the trauma room and quickly exits, pulling her latex gloves off. She comes over and throws the gloves in the trash can next to me, then jabs her hands on her hips.

"I thought Thomas went home," I say sincerely.

"He tried to throw himself in front of a car!" Sarah replies.

Dr. Mattia looks at the floor and laughs after a long moment of silence.

"A moving car, right?" I ask.

Sarah gives me an evil stare. "What do you think?"

I shake my head and laugh. "He said he wants to quit doing cocaine. I think he's more afraid of the people who sold it to him."

Dr. Mattia looks up. "That's just great. I have a drug dealer hiding in my ER."

It's a moment of comradery, a moment of agreement of the facts presented before us. We are unified for a few seconds to the common good of the mental health community and of society as a whole. Quickly it fades away.

"By the way, Doc, the guy in Room Four, well, he's either highly delusional or possessed by the devil. I'm not sure which it is at this point."

He looks directly at me. "I choose delusional."

It's the best choice. Either way, Ronald will be transferred to a mental hospital for further evaluation. A psychiatrist will further sedate him for a few weeks and attempt to open his mind to see what's hiding there. If he is delusional, there might be some hope for a change. If he is possessed by the devil, it will take a lot more than modern western medicine to help him.

Back in the trauma room, I'm leaning on Thomas's bedrail, watching him cry and slobber on himself. He's lying on his side curled up in a fetal position. He looks completely helpless, but I'm not in the mood to be nice. I'm even more motivated to beat him with the IV pole and give him a good reason to be taking up space in the trauma room. Thomas did me a favor by attempting suicide. Now he will be easy to transfer. He didn't meet the criteria before; now he qualifies to get help for further psychiatric evaluation. I still believe he is hiding from someone who wants to kill him. Illegal drugs and death go together.

I hear a scream and watch three nurses run into Michelle's room. Dr. Mattia follows close behind and stands in the doorway. Two security guards push by him. I'm intrigued, so I walk over next to Dr. Mattia and look in. Michelle is on the bed wrestling with all five of them, screaming let me go, let me die, let me masturbate. She is out of her restraints and has IV tubing wrapped around her head and neck.

"What happened?" I ask.

"She tried to hang herself from the examination lamp," Dr. Mattia replies.

I look up at the lamp. It's big and heavy, but it wouldn't support the weight of anyone. It was a pathetic attempt. A ridiculous cry for help. How embarrassing! I'm reminded of a patient who tried to hang himself from a tree branch and the branch broke. The paramedics were laughing when they told us the branch was only two inches in diameter; it bent to the ground before snapping in half. We sent him home.

Suicidal ideations are an epidemic. Emergency rooms are filled with mental health patients that want to kill themselves. All we do is delay the inevitable. If someone is motivated to die, they will find a way.

Within minutes Michelle is tied down again and swearing up a storm. Her mania is remarkable. I can only imagine how severe her depression gets when she cycles the other direction.

"I'll find her a bed at Oakwood Hospital. The psychiatrist will think she's interesting," I say to Dr. Mattia. He nods and goes to his computer to enter notes.

I'm exhausted. I'm on empty. I want to go to my private oasis in Fast Track. I'm hoping my favorite hospital bed is empty. If it's not, I might just get in bed with the patient. Fast Track is shut down for the night, and the hallway is only partially illuminated. It's deserted. It's another world. It's peaceful. It's void of mental patients trying to kill themselves. As I pass by the rooms, all I see is LED lights glowing from the medical equipment. Suddenly the hallway elongates like an accordion, and my room is ten miles away. I'm in slow motion. The walls pulsate and my head spins. I fall against a hospital bed in the hallway. I'm sweating profusely. I think I'm going to vomit. I think I'm going to soil myself. I crawl into the bed and lie in a fetal position, hugging my knees. My clipboard falls on the floor. I'm exhausted physically, mentally, and emotionally. I close my eyes, hoping the emergency room will just go away and leave me alone.

Working as a crisis counselor in an emergency room is a unique job. Many jobs are demanding. Many occupations are difficult. But a plumber doesn't usually have to deal with death threats. And a cashier at a grocery store doesn't have to face demons. Humans are at their worst in an emergency room. They are at the bottom of society. They have lost their right of freedom and free choice. They are animals, unevolved Neanderthals wanting food or another line of cocaine. Of course, there are a few cases where the patient simply lost the struggle to take out IVC papers first. Angry spouses and family members—just tell the magistrate that you are a threat, and law enforcement will give you a free ride to the ER for further evaluation by a guy like me.

What seems like a few seconds passes by, and I open my eyes to look at my watch. It's 6:30 AM. I sit up and throw my legs over the side of the bed. My clipboard is next to me. Someone must have walked by and felt sorry for me. Hopefully it was Sarah or CJ and not Dr. Mattia. Shift change for the staff is at 7:30. I still have until 5:00 PM to counsel the mentally ill. My 72-hour shift is about to kill me, but if I can get home and have a few beers with Leroy and a few hours' sleep, I can make it. A three-day shift isn't unusual for me, but a three-day holiday weekend is.

Today is Labor Day. The mentally ill have an extra day to drink and drug and suffer a meltdown. Self-medicating works well for some, but not so well for others.

I turn my head to listen to the sounds coming from the ER. It's quiet, but it should be at this hour. Acute mental illness typically boils over at 3:00 AM and cools down as the sun rises. The problem with today being a holiday is that a small group of citizens with mental illness and money still in their pockets will wake up this morning and feel an obligation to snort another line, start into a new bottle of booze, or open a fresh 18-pack of beer. Facing reality can wait another day. It's a holiday!

My stomach rumbles. I need a plan of action so I can get out of here. The cafeteria opened thirty minutes ago, and I still have patients to transfer. A hot meal and a gallon of coffee will get me through the morning. I'm not sure who needs to be transferred to a mental hospital yet because if any underlying medical concerns are noted, the patient will be transferred upstairs to the medical floor for further evaluation. If Ronald has high blood pressure, the psychiatrists won't accept the transfer. If Michelle has a urinary tract infection, she won't leave our hospital. Back to supply and demand—the mental hospitals have plenty of business so they can be picky about who they want to treat. They don't treat medical problems.

David walks down the hallway from the ER with a backpack over his shoulder. I don't know him very well, so I'm not sure what to say. I suddenly feel vulnerable and stupid sitting alone in the dark.

"Long night," he says.

"Is Ronald staying, or do I need to find him a bed somewhere?"

David may not have a good answer to that question. I'm being a little sarcastic, and I'm not even sure if he knows the criteria for a mental health transfer.

He stops across from me and leans on the wall. He looks as tired as I feel. It looks like we're going to have a conversation of some kind. I push my glasses up my nose and run my fingers through my soiled hair.

"Dr. Mattia wants to send him upstairs. His blood sugar is high. It's over two hundred."

I can't help but smile. That means I'm done with Ronald. He must have diabetes, but it doesn't explain the odd behavior. Low blood sugar causes bizarre behavior. A 60-year-old grandmother once punched me because of low blood sugar. My jaw was sore for a few days. David keeps talking.

"That guy Thomas who tried to off himself with a car, he went upstairs, too."

I'm counting the minutes until I can have a beer with Leroy. Unless I have a new patient that arrived while I was sleeping, it looks like Michelle is the only patient I need to transfer. She tried to kill herself in the ER, so it shouldn't take long.

"What's wrong with Thomas besides a cocaine habit?" I ask.

"Chest pain."

"Seriously?"

"He started throwing PVCs."

Pre-ventricular contractions, frequently the first sign of a heart attack. Chest pain and difficulty breathing usually accompany the deadly heart rhythm. Put them all together and you might be doing CPR.

David mentions smoking a cigarette together, but I'm in too much of a hurry to get to the phone and transfer Michelle. My feet hit the floor, and I run down the hallway and through the ER. I make no eye contact for fear that someone will need a suicide evaluation or a bed at a detox facility. The first hospital I call finds her interesting and accepts the transfer. I call the sheriff's department for transportation and proceed to run out the door into the parking lot. For a moment, I can't find my yellow Jeep and panic that it was stolen or set on fire. Then I remember, I parked it around the corner near the labor and delivery entrance. I run through the parking lot dodging a few moving cars and find it next to Sarah's Tahoe. Moments later I'm driving along the coast, feeling pretty good about life and fairly confident that I won't have another patient until this afternoon.

It's five o'clock somewhere, so I go to a gas station that sells beer this early and buy a 12-pack. I'm even more confident that there won't be any beer or food in my refrigerator, thanks to Leroy. I inhale the first beer and start into my second one, watching the road closely for any police cars. If I got pulled over, they would know who I was, and probably send me on my way with a warning.

"Hey officer, would you like a cold beer? I still have eight left."

The ER suddenly feels a million miles away, and I'm breathing easier thanks to the alcohol. I reflect on the chaos of last night and wonder how we survive as a species. The only reason we are at the top of the food chain is because humans have an insatiable sex drive. Two people made over seven billion in a few thousand years, after all.

I try to make a connection between Ronald, Thomas, and Michelle, but nothing makes sense. Mental illness, drug abuse, suicidal ideations—maybe the simple answer is that people who have mental illness eventually try to kill themselves and eventually end up talking to me at the ER. I'm on that list. As much as the ER is my prison, it's also my therapy. Talking to someone crazier than myself helps me feel normal. Of course, normal is just a statistical average. Maybe the average person is the one we should all be afraid of.

TWELVE

I turn off the Jeep and sit in silence for a few minutes, finishing another cold beer. I normally have a lot more self-control, but it's been a long and crazy weekend at the ER. Plus, as much as I enjoy Leroy's company, it's always less stressful if you visit him in Florida. Clothes everywhere and no food in the house, it's the same domestic experience if you go to his place, but now I'm faced with having to vacuum the ceiling and scrub three bathrooms with a toothbrush. My OCD is running off the charts.

My condominium appears quiet. I glance at Leroy's pickup truck, and it has at least ten golf clubs leaning on it. I'm not sure if he was selling his clubs or maybe washed them and forgot what he was doing. Fortunately, my immediate neighbors are honest. Only Rick might take some interest, and he would return the clubs after using them for a few days.

I get out of the Jeep to gather the empty beer cans I threw in the backseat when I notice Susan looking out her door. Susan is my neighbor opposite of Rick. She leans around the door and waves at me. I wave back. It's still early, so I'm surprised anyone but me is awake. Maybe she is getting ready for church. No, wait, it's Monday.

"Hey, Susan."

"A long night at work?"

"Pretty crazy for sure."

"I was wondering if you could help me move a couch?"

A couch? I look at my watch. It's not even 8:00 AM.

It must be nice to have nothing better to worry about. She probably lost a lot of sleep wondering where to move the couch. Susan is retired or disabled, I'm not sure which. We've never gotten beyond an occasional hello in the parking lot. She's old enough to be my mother.

"Um, sure," I respond reluctantly.

She opens the door and invites me into her living room. The couch isn't very big, but what concerns me most is she is wearing a nightgown, and it's see-through. Suddenly I'm having a flashback to my childhood when I first saw my mother in underwear. I try to think of an excuse to run out the front door.

I grab hold of the couch and start to drag it across the floor.

"Where do you want it?"

Susan hurries to pick up the other end before I break something.

"In the bedroom," she answers.

Who puts a couch in the bedroom?

As quickly as I can, I maneuver the couch into the narrow hallway leading to the bedroom. Her condominium is similar to mine, so I'm having doubts this is even going to work. After wrestling with it for a few minutes, and getting it stuck in the door, I drop my end on the floor and put my hands in the air in defeat. Susan is on the other end, trapped in the bedroom. She suddenly looks concerned.

"This isn't going to work!" I erupt.

"But I had it in here before."

"Well…I have to go to the bathroom." And with that I nearly run out of her condo and into mine. I close and lock the door behind me, hoping I won't see her again. It's strangely dark inside, and I see that Leroy has blankets draped over the curtains. He even has a bath towel covering the window over the sink. I doubt it's a clean towel. I remember he brought it with him.

I see OB coming at me and suddenly his nose is in my crotch. I push him away and go to the refrigerator. I open a can of beer and Leroy wakes up. He is sleeping on a mattress on the floor in the living room.

"Breakfast?"

"How much are you selling your five-iron for, Leroy?"

I look in the refrigerator and see the remains of a pizza. I wasn't aware anyone delivered out here.

"Where did this pizza come from?"

Leroy laughs. Evidently there is a story behind it. I wonder if Eddie is involved again.

"Mama Mia's pizza."

It's a pizza place a few miles down the road. They definitely don't deliver. Leroy was out drinking and driving for sure.

"Do you need to go to detox, Leroy? I could probably find you a bed somewhere."

Leroy comes into the kitchen in his underwear. At least he's not naked.

"I'll go if you go." He opens one of my beers. "Did you see any crazy people last night?"

The kitchen is a good place for casual conversation. Having food and refreshments so close is comforting to anyone. I lean on the counter and take a long pull on my can, then belch for good measure.

"It's amazing how screwed up people are, Leroy."

"That bad, huh?"

"We're doing pretty good for ourselves, Leroy."

He laughs. "Well, let me know when we're not."

A few minutes later, Leroy is on the back patio chipping balls into a bucket he put in the fairway. He is still in his underwear but is somewhat hidden by the short privacy walls. As long as he doesn't leave the patio, I probably won't get a complaint against me. I do my best to hide from Eddie and his rules. Hopefully no one is playing this early because it would be difficult to locate your ball in the sea of balls Leroy has scattered across the fairway.

After finding Scar sound asleep under my bed, I take a quick shower and meet Leroy outside for some golf. He is waiting for me in a golf cart and has beers strategically placed so he can drink and drive as well as golf and drink. I'm done with my shift in about eight hours and instead of eating a good meal and getting some sleep, I'm going to hang out with Leroy and receive some therapy. Leroy has a unique solution to everything.

"Did you tell Eddie you were looking for OB again?"

"No. We paid for it this time. I charged it to your account."

"Account?"

"Sure. At the clubhouse."

"I didn't know I had a charge account?"

"I have a charge account at fifty golf courses in Florida. Just pay the minimum and keep them happy. It's interest free that way."

Another unique solution.

We play three balls for three holes and go around twice. It only takes us an hour. According to Leroy, that's eighteen holes. I try to count his beers, but I lose track after twelve. Not surprising, Leroy has a stash of beer in a cooler on the back patio. He doesn't venture far from his liquid courage. Golf, beer, and sleep: Leroy has a charmed life. It's simplicity on a new level. He eats tuna out of the can and spends little money on anything. His social network is limited, and as long as he doesn't spend the night, he's a good friend to have around.

We pull up to the condo to unload the clubs. OB walks through the open screen door to meet us. I pick up an empty can.

"Should we leave these in the cart for Eddie to clean up?"

"Sure. I do it all the time."

I drop the can in my yard. "Problem is, only beer purchased at the clubhouse is allowed to be consumed on the golf course."

"No shit?" I have his attention now.

"And he charges a lot for beer," I add.

"Eddie is a land shark," Leroy concludes after some thought. He opens another beer and litters the yard with an empty can.

I wonder how long the cans will lie there if I don't pick them up. Leroy has just challenged me to a duel, a mental wrestling match. He knows I have OCD. I'm going to lose for sure.

"Maybe one of the mowers will pick them up?" I reply.

Leroy is proud of his littering skills. I'm going to get an eviction notice for sure. And most of my neighbors didn't pay attention to me before this weekend.

"I like it," Leroy says, then goes inside with OB. I'm left with the golf cart and a warm beer in my hand.

I look at my watch. It's almost noon. I'm finished with my 72-hour shift in five hours. It's Monday and a holiday. The afternoon is unpredictable at best. The ER will be off the chain tonight for sure, but it won't be my problem, and I'm just hoping for an easy afternoon. I have beer in my belly and rocks in my head, so I'm not much good to anyone right now. The stress of counseling homicidal and suicidal patients got the best of me. I should be sleeping or at least resting so I can do my job. I think of Ronald possessed by a demon and Michelle trying to hang herself with IV tubing.

My cell phone rings. It's the ER.

"This is Stewart."

"Dr. Guda has a few patients he would like for you to see. When can we expect you?"

"Umm…I'll be there in forty-five minutes. I'm at home right now."

"I will let him know."

A few means two or more. Sometimes the ER doctors wait until there is a line of mental patients before calling me. They think they are doing me a favor by waiting. No matter how bad it gets this afternoon, I'm comforted knowing I can sleep in my own bed tonight. My electric bed in the Fast Track hallway will have to be used by another patient. Hopefully no one will die in my room this week.

❊ ❊ ❊

I look up from my clipboard at my next patient. Her name is Ann, and she's 26 years old. She came in voluntarily for suicidal ideations secondary to crack cocaine abuse. She admitted to smoking cocaine four times or more a day for the past three months.

"That's a lot of cocaine, Ann."

The hospital bed is upright, and she's pressed against it, nervous and agitated. She looks like she's ready to run out the door. The bedsheet is bunched in her hands, and I noticed her clothes are dirty and her shoes are torn.

She looks at me. "I don't care about myself anymore. I used to be pretty."

No response is sometimes the best response.

"I don't care about my safety. I'll go anywhere and do anything to get high. I frequently have sex with strangers. I wake up in bed, and I don't know who is next to me. Sometimes there's more than one person sleeping next to me."

I might be old fashioned, but that's disgusting. The reckless exchange of body fluids is a playground for sexually transmitted diseases.

"I have four children that I don't care about," she adds.

I break eye contact with her and flip through the pages in her chart. She has no formal diagnosis for mental illness and no history of ER visits. Her blood alcohol level was .20, and her urine drug screen was positive for about everything.

"Where are your children right now?"

She hesitates. "I think I left them with my mother...a few days ago."

It's unusual to see a parent, a mother, so detached from her family. I don't usually get involved with a patient's family, other than interviewing them to uncover sordid information, but the fact that she isn't sure where her children are scares me. Unfortunately, sexual predators are everywhere. The average person doesn't consider such a threat. It's real, and it's even possible her children's safety has already been compromised. Maybe her mother is passed out drunk, and the new boyfriend is playing doctor. I'll ask one of the nurses to contact DSS.

"Do you want to kill yourself, Ann? You are doing a pretty good job so far." My voice is ice cold. I surprise myself.

She grips the bedsheet harder and stares straight ahead. "If you let me go, I'll overdose on pills. I'm warning you. I have the pills at home, and I'll do it!"

I sit back in the chair and try to think of an appropriate response. I will talk to Dr. Guda and get you released as soon as possible, is my first thought. On the other hand, Ann is here asking for help. Seems she doesn't want to take that next step. She could have overdosed already.

"What kind of pills, Ann?"

"Sleeping pills."

"I will talk to Dr. Guda. You aren't capable of taking care of yourself or anyone else at this point." I stand up to go. My words are lethal like daggers. Ann is vulnerable like all ER patients. I have to be careful. I have to be kind, even though I don't want to be. I understand recreational drug and alcohol usage. I can't sympathize with someone who makes it their full-time job.

"I will try to find out where your children are, Ann."

I leave her in silence and go to Dr. Guda.

"Hey, Doc. The cocaine abuser in Room Four needs IVC papers taken out."

Dr. Guda bows to me, as if I'm someone special. We work well together. Mental patients don't wait long in the ER when we are both on duty. Our goal is the same: move patients along and keep beds available for real emergencies. I laugh in response.

"Do you want to take out the papers, Doc? I'll let you borrow my Jeep."

"No. And I can't fit into those things. I'm too big." He rubs his belly.

"Who else do you have for me?" I ask, looking at my watch.

He points to different rooms. "There's an eleven-year-old who told her therapist she wants to die, and an eighteen-year-old male who chased his family through the house with a butcher knife."

"A butcher knife? I've never owned a real butcher knife," I reply.

"Me neither. I buy my steaks already cut."

"I'm off at five o'clock, Doc. I'll try to clear these people out before then. I'm finishing a seventy-two-hour shift."

He takes a deep breath. "That's nuts. I sure hope you get paid well."

If he only knew. My employer is crazier than most of my patients.

"I'm headed to the magistrate, Doc. I'll be back shortly."

"Take your time, Stewart."

Time is finally on my side. It's 1:30 PM when I pull out of the parking lot and drive south along the coast to the courthouse. Ann needs an involuntary commitment order because she is a danger to herself. She came in voluntarily but could leave at any time to go eat a bottle of pills. A signed order from the magistrate, an after-hours judge, is what I need. Magistrates are typically available 24/7 to do things judges don't like to do, like marry people and set bond for new crimes committed. As I said, if you are mad at someone, go to a magistrate and say they are suicidal. Chances are the sheriff will arrest them and take them to the ER to talk to someone like me. It will be unpleasant at best.

I'm in luck, the magistrate is Harry Parker. Harry is a retired sheriff's deputy and hates mental patients. Harry opens the door to his office, bypassing the bullet-proof glass and cameras. I sit down and wait for the paperwork to print.

"I can't understand these cokeheads," he starts the conversation.

"This lady doesn't even know where her kids are. She has four of them."

"God Almighty. What's our society coming to? Someone is going to blow us off the map if we keep spending tax dollars on these idiots." He pounds a fist on the desk.

"I feel ya, Harry. Do you remember in H. G. Wells' *The Time Machine* when the horn would blow and everyone would march into the incinerators?"

"That would be a great job. I would do it for free."

"I think a lot of people would volunteer to walk into the incinerator," I add.

We both think about it. "That's weird. I wonder why?" he replies.

"I have a theory, Harry. Do you want to hear it?"

"I'm not sure."

"Well, I think there are only two kinds of people."

"Okay."

"Hosts and parasites."

He signs the IVC papers, and a woman comes into the lobby and steps up to the bullet-proof window.

"May I help you?" Harry inquires.

"Yes. My husband is a worthless drunk, and I want him out of my house."

Harry looks at me. "Is this one of yours?"

I get up to leave. "He might be if he stays with her."

Harry smiles. "Have a good week off, Stewart. I'll see you next weekend, I'm sure."

Back at the ER, I check in with the charge nurse to see if I have any new patients. The ER staff is unfamiliar to me because it's a weekday and a holiday. Most of them are part-timers, trying to make some extra money. I'm moving fast, drinking coffee, making calls, giving reports, entering my narratives, and my goal is to clear my patients out of the ER by five o'clock. What happens after that isn't my business.

❋ ❋ ❋

"Hannah, my name is Stewart. Dr. Guda wanted me to talk to you."

Hannah is 11 years old. She's the youngest patient I've ever had, although I frequently see teenagers in the ER ruminating about death. It's usually a girl with a broken heart.

Hannah is nicely dressed and appears well nourished. She's sitting up in bed watching cartoons.

"Could you turn off *SpongeBob*, so we can talk?"

I'm giving her control over the conversation.

She turns off the TV. She looks bored with me already.

"I like Patrick. He and I have a lot in common," I say.

"Why?" She responds like I'm stupid.

"Because he's simple-minded and he eats a lot of junk."

Hannah gives me a slight nod. She's obviously a smart kid. It would take some real manipulation of adults to wind up at the ER for acute mental illness. She apparently told her therapist this morning that she would rather be dead.

She's 11 and she already has a therapist.

I decide to be blunt. Handling her gently is what everyone probably does.

"So, do you want to kill yourself?"

"Like suicide?"

"That's one approach."

"What else is there?"

"Well, you could join the Marines and get sent to Afghanistan."

"I'm too young."

"Wait a few years; it could happen."

She smiles at the possibility.

"I already told Dr. Guda I'm not suicidal."

"Words are cheap, Hannah. Maybe Patrick and I really don't have anything in common."

"Then how would you know if I'm really suicidal?"

I just opened a can of worms. She's good at being philosophical, and I don't have the time. She needs to go home and find another therapist. I'll give her five minutes to vent some frustration. I look at my watch.

"You might be suicidal, but this is an emergency room. We see people all the time that complain of suicidal thoughts. And do you know what we do with them?"

"What?"

"We listen to them and send them home."

She falls silent. Hannah appears disappointed.

"The people that don't go home are the ones who put guns in their mouths and handfuls of pills in their stomachs. Hangings are common—we had a lady try to hang herself here last night."

"What?" She is amazed.

"Sure. Climbed up on her bed, wrapped IV tubing around her neck, and tried to hang herself from an examination lamp."

"Wasn't anyone watching her?"

I pause, knowing she will never forget this conversation. "We had her tied to the bed, but she got loose."

Hannah's eyes grow big. If she did have suicidal ideations this morning, she now has a better perspective on her depression. She now sees the possibilities ahead and her current placement on the mental illness ladder. Is it dangerous to share this information with a patient? Maybe she will go home and look for a gun. Probably not. It's more important that she stays out of the ER unless she has a real problem. It's my job to keep beds open. We don't need any more business around here.

After talking to her mother about finding a good psychiatrist who might prescribe some medication, I also suggested she find a new therapist she could trust. Her therapist wasn't able to read Hannah's feelings correctly because Hannah wasn't sharing her thoughts completely.

I staff with the nurses, then go to the phones to find a bed for Michelle. A few minutes later, I hear Rascal Flats coming from Shelly's desk. She might know something more about the patient with the butcher knife.

"Have you ever chased someone with a butcher knife?" I ask, leaning on a file cabinet. Shelly is wired on caffeine as usual.

"No, but I once chased my sister around the house with a pair of scissors."

"To give her a haircut maybe?"

"I wanted to stab her. I was mad."

"Apparently so." The conversation just went sideways. "What about the guy in Room Eight?"

"His family brought him in." She pulls up a record on the screen. "Looks like he shops for hospitals."

I count the number of ER visits he's had in the last year. I stop at ten.

"Wow. I wonder what he's shopping for?"

"Probably pain pills."

Shelly has little medical training, but it's a good assumption. It's not a crime to go to the local ER and lie about pain or anxiety. You don't even need insurance. Someone will set you up on a payment plan, and you don't have to pay the bill if you don't want to. Not everyone cares about a good credit score.

I enter the ER through the family room and go to the nurses' station. I still don't recognize anyone on the staff, but that gives me some freedom to relax. No one here knows I have OCD or diarrhea, and only Dr. Guda has seen me in my yellow Jeep. The nurses are busy, and I have a moment to read Paul's chart. He is 18 years old and has a part-time job of going to the ER. He wants something, but no one is giving it to him. Plus, he chased his family around the house with a butcher knife.

I look up at the admission board. Another patient with mental illness just arrived.

THIRTEEN

"Where did you get the butcher knife?"
"From the kitchen."
I'm still fascinated that he even found a butcher knife.
"Did you hurt anyone?"
"No. I just wanted to scare them."
"Why?"

It's a valid question. Terrorizing family members in your home is unusual and unkind. Paul either does this for fun or he's desperately trying to gain control of the situation. I'm trying to keep in mind that he's had this conversation many times before. I look out into the ER and see a sheriff's deputy walking to the nurses' station. The IVC papers I took out on Ann just gave us authority over her personal safety. She just lost all her legal rights.

Paul thinks long and hard about his response. The silence causes me some concern, and I watch him closely. He is sitting up in bed, hugging his knees and rocking back and forth. Paul has glasses and looks slightly malnourished.

"I can't understand why my family keeps bringing me here?"
"Here, like to the ER?"
"Yes. I think they might be poisoning me."

Paul hasn't looked at me yet, even though I've done everything to gain his attention, including dismantling my pen and making weird noises. He appears to be watching the activity in the ER, but he might be just staring at nothing.

Poison?

Back to the problem with the butcher knife. "Do you think you are angry at your family for something, Paul?"

"Sometimes when I get angry, I'm not sure what I'm going to do next."

"Do you hear voices? Not like mine, but inside your head?"

"Yes."

"What do the voices tell you?"

"To kill everyone."

"Everyone, like your family?"

"The whole world."

Homicidal ideations are less common than suicidal ideations. Killing yourself is a lot easier than killing others. People fight back.

"I understand how you feel, Paul." Maybe no one has ever told him that. "I wish I could blow up the world," I add.

"Yeah!" he nearly screams, then begins a fit of laughter, still rocking back and forth.

Tangential thinking, looseness of associations, and delusional thinking—Paul is a mess. We can't send him home in this condition. He might chop up his family with a butcher knife.

"Why do you think you are being poisoned, Paul?"

His answer doesn't really matter. I will instruct the family to take out IVC papers at the magistrate. Paul needs further psychiatric support. He is currently a danger to society. Anyhow, it will give Harry something to do.

Paul stops rocking. He looks directly at me. I stand up.

"I'm going to kill you too, Stewart."

I leave in a hurry and walk past the deputy. "Keep your eye on him, Bill. He's nuts!"

"Aren't they all," he laughs and shoves a piece of gum in his mouth.

I go to the phones and relax for a few minutes, soaking in the solitude and subtle mood lighting. It's not always quiet in the reception area, but thanks to the holiday, today it is. Patients are going to the other side, checking in with Shelly.

Paul scared me because he addressed me by name. I don't even remember telling him my name. Plus, he said he is going to kill me, not would kill me, or might kill me. I'll have to start sleeping with a gun again.

I nearly fall asleep in my chair and wake up suddenly when my clipboard hits the floor. I have to keep moving. One more patient so far. Just one more interview to go. No new admissions showing. The bottom will fall out tonight for sure, but I don't care. Soon I'll be driving home, following the coastline in my yellow Jeep, drinking a cold beer. It's the end of a long weekend, and anyone with even the slightest substance abuse problem or mental health issue will want to visit the ER for a friendly chat, and I won't be there.

I go to Shelly with obvious excitement in my voice. "Hey, who's the psych patient in Room Eight? I've got a date with a twelve-pack of beer and a guy named Leroy."

"Gross!" She doesn't look away from her computer screen.

I lean over the counter and glance down the hallway toward the front entrance. Numerous people are sitting in the reception area, but no one appears mentally unstable.

"It's Marshall Winston," Shelly replies.

"No way!" I nearly scream.

"He was here this weekend already."

"He lives here!" I yell down the hallway, as I disappear through the automatic doors into the ER.

"Marshall, it's good to see you!"

He startles and stands up as I barge into the room. Marshall appears intoxicated and loses his balance, stumbling into an exam tray and knocking assorted supplies to the floor. I grab his arm to steady him. A nurse appears in the doorway.

"Everything alright in here?"

"Just a friendly dance. Marshall, why don't you sit down."

The nurse leaves, and I help Marshall into the chair. He must be in a hurry to go somewhere because he is using the chair instead of the bed, and he has a suitcase with him. His face is red and he appears agitated.

I see Marshall more than any ten patients combined. My immediate concern is he doesn't look like he wants to go home. He wants us to save him from his own demons. He wants the honest taxpayers to put him in a nice detox facility with a warm bed and three hot meals a day, so he won't have the luxury of drinking himself to death in his own home.

I'm only happy to see him because it's easy to deny him inpatient treatment due to noncompliance, which means we can feed him a meal, sober him up, and send him home. Dr. Guda will be glad to see him leave.

I see no need to talk to Marshall. It's the same old story about being tired of drinking and wanting to sober up. The only way Marshall is going to sober up is if we keep a guard on him 24/7 for the rest of his life. But why bother? He's not special. He doesn't contribute anything to society. Marshall is one of thousands sharing the same lifestyle, spending their disability checks on alcohol and weighing down the healthcare system.

I put out my hand to shake his. "I'll talk to Dr. Guda, Marshall."

I leave the room and go to finish my notes. Admissions is suddenly busy. I hear Shelly say I've got another one coming in.

"Thank you!" I respond without any concern. It's after 5:00 PM and the next crisis counselor will have to take the call. My three-day, 72-hour shift is over, and I'm still alive. I've battled diarrhea, malnutrition, insomnia, OCD, and Leroy, and I'm feeling pretty good.

"Who's the guy in Room Eight?"

I recognize the voice and spin my chair around. "Felicity!"

"You look awful," she replies.

"And I feel even worse. It's Marshall Winston."

"That drunk! Let me talk to him." She puts her briefcase down.

"I already did. He has his suitcase packed and wants a room somewhere."

"Let's just send him home. He's not a threat to anyone and he's never suicidal. I'll ask Dr. Guda for some Ativan."

Felicity is a good crisis counselor. She doesn't play around. I take the time, maybe too much time, to talk to people. Felicity gets right to the diagnosis. She doesn't discuss much.

"Marshall told the nurse he's been drinking all weekend. He apparently drank three forty-ounce beers and four bottles of wine since yesterday, but who knows when yesterday was, right?"

Felicity digs through her briefcase and finds a lighter and cigarette. "I'm going to smoke this, then get to work."

"Just twelve hours?" I laugh.

"All week long, just nights. Are you working this next weekend?"

"Yes. The chaos should be back to normal by then," I respond.

She leaves but comes back, poking her head around the door frame. "How many patients did you see this weekend, Stewart?"

I let out a long, jagged breath. "I'm not sure, Felicity. I lost track of time Saturday morning about four AM."

"Get some rest." She smiles, then leaves.

I go home to drink beer with Leroy, only to find he has left town. A note written on a piece of paper bag and duct-taped to my refrigerator says he is on his way to Ohio to play golf. The doors are closed and the condo smells like a dog. It will take me a week to sterilize everything. Scar will have to start following the house rules again: keep the sandbox clean and no butt rubs on the carpet.

The following morning, I drive to Jacksonville to try to collect my paycheck. I can't keep working without pay. My employer doesn't know much about what I do. It's a mental health corporation that manages a menagerie of treatments, providing anything from mental health education to hospice. They own nursing homes and counseling agencies and somehow got involved in the after-hours crisis contract at my emergency room. The money to be made by billing Medicaid is attractive. Unfortunately, somebody mishandled the finances in the corporate office. Felicity told me they might be bankrupt. Our contract changes hands frequently because Medicaid doesn't like to pay, but they do like to change their billing policies and force the paper machine to a standstill. They save money if no one can submit a bill. Meanwhile, crazy people continue to pour in. Patients have no idea who pays who, and they couldn't care less. A warm meal, two milligrams of Ativan, and temporary shelter from their demons is what matters.

When I arrive at their office, I'm met by two sheriff's deputies. It's 9:00 AM, and I look forward to enjoying a relaxing week with some money and without any disturbances. My condo on the golf course will get sterilized, and I can happily stare out the window in silence, counting the leaves on the trees or the blades of grass around the sand trap. OCD has its membership requirements.

"Good morning, officers. What's up?"

I don't expect an answer. It's just a figure of speech.

"Just here to keep the peace."

I don't know either one of them. This isn't my county. I'm away from my jurisdiction. I check in with the receptionist, and she asks me if I would like to sit down.

"No. I'll just stand," I reply.

I walk back to the deputies to see why they are there. Before I have the chance to ask, one of them asks, "Are you Stewart?"

My stomach turns and my throat gets tight. I remember my words, which have come back to haunt me, "Don't make me drive ninety miles. You will be sorry."

"Now, wait a minute, guys. I'm, I'm…these people owe me money. I've been working without a paycheck for three weeks!" I whisper as loud as I can.

I'm waiting to be handcuffed. I'm going to spend the rest of my life in a Mexican prison eating cockroaches.

"Just get your money and go," one of them replies.

I get my paycheck and drive away feeling abused. All the hard work I put into helping the acutely mentally ill, and now I'm not sure where my next paycheck is coming from. They didn't fire me. They didn't reprimand me. They said the ER contract was going to change hands again. I would need to speak to the new mental health conglomerate about employment. Here's a 1-800 number you can call.

It's a hot sunny day. Labor Day weekend has come and gone, and for most people it was uneventful. But for a small population labeled mentally ill, it was traumatizing. Too much time, too much heat, and too much alcohol—it's a perfect recipe for a mental meltdown.

I drive north along the coastline past bird sanctuaries and salt marshes, admiring the oversized homes and expensive boats docked in the back yards. The rich are getting richer and the poor are growing sicker. The wealthy and healthy try their best to ignore the mentally ill, looking the other way, tossing coins into cans, locking doors, and turning up music at stoplights. But mental America can't be ignored. Our society enables mental illness. Runaway capitalism and free enterprise naturally leave the weak behind. Other species eliminate their sick. We support our weakest members and call it religion or public assistance.

But who am I to have any solutions? I'm just good at talking to homicidal and suicidal people. I counsel people at their worst. I help clean up the mess our society makes at the local emergency room.

I am a mop and bucket.

I decide it would be a good day to put the top down on the yellow Jeep. I pull off the road and get the owner's manual out to make sure I do it right. It's rather simple as I soon realize. Back on the road with the sun's rays beating down on me and dirt and fumes blowing everywhere, I put on my sunglasses and force a smile.

And then I think about Leroy. Maybe he is right after all. Maybe Leroy does have a sustainable recipe for lasting mental health—play lots of free golf, keep your life simple, and worry about absolutely nothing.

The End

Made in United States
Cleveland, OH
10 August 2025